BE LOVE

JENNAFER WHITE

To Brady. Every day, you make me realize you could have done way better.

CONTENTS

CHAPTER 1

HOW DO YOU DO?

Welcome. Welcome to my book. As you may know from the cover, I'm Jennafer. You are about to read many pages devoted to events, people, and balloons (yes, there will be balloons!) from my past, so I thought you might like to know what I'm doing right now in the present.

Well, at the moment I write this, I'm a whopping two years into my thirties. I am married and own a dog. I live just down the road from Cinderella Castle, a.k.a. Orlando, Florida. Like many of my fellow Orlandoans, my paycheck comes in from Mickey Mouse and goes immediately out to pay my mortgage. In general, I'm just your average millennial young adult living in the two-thousand-teens. I think I know more than I do, and I spend far too much time searching for the next great Candy Crush on my iPhone.

So what am I doing writing a book? I should have no use for books. But it turns out that I do have a very particular use for books and look, if you needed proof, you're holding the book in your hands (thank you, btw). The purpose of this book is to give you a message. What message?

We'll get to that.

Back in the early days of thinking about this book, I remember calling my brother-in-law and telling him about an idea God laid on my heart. I told my brother-in-law that this idea kept pressing in on me—to write a series of short stories. As I held the phone explaining this idea, nerves caused my mouth to fill with cotton. Finally, I choked out my question: would he be willing to edit this college-credits-but-no-degree girl's book? Thank goodness he agreed.

See, I never thought of myself as the book-writing type, but I couldn't avoid this push God was giving me. I felt a very specific need to write and a very specific purpose for this book.

I wrote this book to encourage you. To let you know, "Hey friend, don't worry, there is someone out there messing up more than you. You're going to make it. You are going to be okay. You don't have to have everything figured out. You don't have to win at all things. Just figure out what God is going to use you for TODAY, and run with it."

I wrote this because I've had the opportunity to witness and play a part in the dizzying heights of some incredible celebrations, the beyond-dark depths of grief, and some eye-popping surprises. I've been blessed to find myself in a few unique and truly special jobs, and I wanted to share with you how humbling these experiences have been. I want you to know how grateful I am to God that he put me in jobs where I could serve and proclaim Jesus' name boldly even in a workplace that isn't fond of "religion."

I wrote this book because I do life a little differently. And I always felt like I wasn't good enough or that I was doing it all wrong. So I wanted to put this out there because maybe you feel the same way. Maybe I have a story you can relate to. Or, maybe there's a story that sparks an idea that you can leg-shimmy about in your own life. (Everyone should shimmy their legs more.)

This is a story for you, no matter how much you feel like a princess or a pauper. No matter where you are right now in life, I want to meet you there, and if I could, I would sit down and have way too much caffeine with you.

You see, if you've been around a church or youth group or even listened to a vaguely Christian podcast, you've heard that "every part of the body of Christ is unique and important." I heard that too, but I never trusted it. We might praise the preacher and the singer and the missionary, but we don't praise *every* part. Not every part fits into a shareable, inspirational, Facebook Live Post. Not every part of the body of Christ is happy-go-lucky, or even happy-go-blessed, if you don't like the lucky word. And here's the kicker: not every part looks the same.

I'm the awkward parts. I'm the shy and timid parts. I'm the parts that have fallen off and are stuck back on with hot glue. But I'm also the sparkly parts. I bet you didn't think we would be talking about "parts" this much in a Christian book, huh? Well, buckle up because more surprises will be headed your way!

Guess what? It doesn't matter which part you play. The message I need to deliver to you through this book is this: You're needed, you're valued, and you are important, EXACTLY where you are today.

Your parts are special.

I promise. And so does He.

CHAPTER 2

BRADY

When I reference my husband throughout these stories, I will simply call him "Brady." Sure, I'll call him that because it's his name, but it's not just a name to me.

His name is the first thing I knew about him. But now, though, after years of knowing the man behind the name, when I hear the word "Brady," I feel ... well, I feel like those women on YouTube falling to the ground after Elvis handed them his sweat towel. (BTW: gross ... Elvis is amazing ... but gross.)

Mothers everywhere with boys named Brady, beware: when I see a pint-sized Brady in the supermarket, I have to restrain myself from wrapping that kid in my arms and inhaling the top of his head. Why? I am convinced that every small boy named Brady has a head that smells like love muffins fresh out of the oven. Of course, I wouldn't do that because of laws and general human decency, but you get the idea. I hear the name and it triggers something in me. Maybe there's an easier way to put it.

I love Brady. Simply that.

But, actually, it's not simple at all. Brady is the boss. He is my biggest cheerleader, biggest supporter, and, at times, my biggest obstacle—the kind of obstacle that pushes me to be better. Most importantly, though, for better or worse, he is mine. That's a weird thing about marriage: you walk down an aisle, you sign a paper, and BAM!—no matter what you do, what smells come out of you (literally last night, Brady lovingly told me the carbon dioxide coming out of my mouth smelled so horrible he could feel it sinking to the bottom of his lungs and scratching his throat on the way down. ... This is love, people. ... Which brings me to my next point): what ugly words you thrash around toward the other person, they have to stay with you. For better or for worse.

Luckily, with Brady, it is more often for the better. Brady is easy-going, level-headed, wise, slow to speak, quick to love, and doesn't super care what others think. I am the opposite of all these things, so I would like to say we balance each other out, but in reality ... I just strive to be more like him every day. And in a lot of ways that means I'm striving to be more like Jesus every day, which probably is what God intended marriage to look like. Maybe.

·····

Now you know his name, you know I feel like hugging strange children, and you know Brady is awesome; but let's rewind to the beginning.

I was fifteen when I first saw Brady. That first glimpse happened at what you might call a wicked-awesome youth conference. I found myself in Branson, Missouri for Young Christian's Weekend at the Silver Dollar City theme park. This conference is big on rollercoasters, funnel cakes, Jesus, fried food, and (most importantly) Christian t-shirts. I love Christian t-shirts with everything inside of me. Give me a good Christian pun, and I am a happy kid. Give me a good Christian pun I can WEAR? I'm done for.

There I was in an amphitheater crowd of 4,000 slightly sweaty religious pun-wearing teens when Brady appeared on stage to play the guitar. Brady came on after his dad, Joe White, had just blown my mind with an epic purity talk (how many of these do we hear as kids? Apparently not enough). Brady stepped out on stage, wearing worn-in jeans and carrying a guitar. I never thought of myself as one of those girls who fell for boys with guitars, but there I was, sitting in the middle of my yellow-matching-shirts-wearing youth group, falling hard for this stranger carrying a musical instrument.

He began to play and to sing the words that would later become my anthem. It was a song that Brady wrote called "Picture of a Wedding."

[Obviously, you have heard this song before and have listened to it on repeat numerous times. ... But in case you need a copy of the lyrics, call me "Genie" because your wish is my command]:

White flowing dress, like the moon upon the water
Catches the wind, as she floats passed her kin
She's a perfect picture of innocence and grace
Light catches her eye, as it moves across her face

Her eyes are fixed upon the man standing there
Deep in her heart she knows that he's the one
All her life she's prayed for

Walking beside her, daddy holds her hand
About to give her away to another man
He looks deep in her eyes, puts a kiss upon her cheek

I love my princess, forgive me if I weep

He turns his eyes to the boy standing there
Deep in his heart he knows that boy's the one
All her life he's prayed for

Standing tall a little weak at the knees
The words don't come so the Lord intercedes
All of his life, he's been waiting for this day
The sight of his bride, took his breath away

And he's in awe by the angel there
Deep in his heart he knows that girl's the one
All his life he's prayed for

Looking down from heaven, a tear in His eye
Look at this picture, and know why I died
A boy and a girl with purity of heart
I give you my blessing for I know that you'll never ever part

I loved that song. I instantly loved Brady White.

My friend and I went together to buy Brady's CD (she paid $6, I paid $4—which meant I got the illegally-burned copy of the CD when we got home. … What foreshadowing of Brady's future … his wife just stealing things from him all the time). On the way home from the conference, I placed the copy of his CD into my blue Discman and listened to his voice the whole five-hour charter bus ride home. I leaned over to my hilarious friend, Kelly Slater. I whispered into her ear, "Someday, I will marry Brady White."

But that Someday would not come for quite some time.

* * * * *

A few years later, my Aunt Sara hired Brady to perform at a youth retreat. She spent the whole weekend telling Brady about her amazing niece, Jennafer, who worked at Walt Disney World. My incredible sidekick younger cousins placed pictures of me all around the room where Brady slept (which he claims he didn't notice—rude), and thus began Brady's weekend of brainwashing. My family rules.

At the time of this "brainwashing visit," I was doing a College Program internship at Disney World. I spent my intern days as a ride attendant at The Great Movie Ride (which is the greatest attraction Disney World has to offer, in my humble opinion). I was decked out in my Cast Member costume when Aunt Sara called.

"I am pretty sure you're going to marry Brady White," she predicted. "He is older than you, and you're young. So I've begun praying that God would prepare your heart. I think you're going to get married young."

I knew I was going to marry Brady when I was 15. Now Aunt Sara knew it as well, and then as God would have it, I saw Brady again a few months later.

He was playing at the same Young Christian's Weekend event where I'd first heard him play "Picture of a Wedding." I was now chaperoning the same youth group I came to know Jesus through when I was kid. I sat in a conference room surrounded by friends and family and anxiously awaited my betrothed's (even though he didn't know it yet) arrival.

Brady walked into the room, and my heart stopped. I was a youth group chaperone and former Great Movie Ride attendant, and here in front of me was this cool musician I'd only seen from afar and heard about. He had a guitar and he loved Jesus and he had a green shirt on and his hair swooped perfectly and I was in love.

We were introduced, had a perfect meet-cute, and when I walked into my hotel room later that night, Sara and the other chaperones from the trip put a makeshift pillowcase veil on my head and serenaded me with "Goin' To The Chapel."

That was March 31st, 2006. Ten months later, I would walk down the aisle to meet that perfectly-swooped hair at the altar and change my last name to White.

I guess you could say "God answers prayers," or "GAP"; at least, that's what I read on a Christian t-shirt one time.

CHAPTER 3

OUR FIRST FIGHT

When Brady and I were engaged, we liked to cook dinner together in my apartment and then save the world. I suppose to be more honest, I should say that after dinner we binge-watched Jack Bauer saving the world 24 hours at a time.

This was way back in the prehistoric days pre-Netflix and Hulu. We didn't have streaming in those days; we binge-watched like our forefathers: physically driving to a store buying actual DVDs and putting them in the player one at a time. Truthfully, the words "binge" and "watch" probably hadn't even met yet. Wait ... did Brady and I invent "binge-watching"? We must have. We are so accomplished. These were dark, dark times, people.

One night, we ate and started to unload the dishwasher. Every single dish in the dishwasher was super wet, and we couldn't figure out why. Brady tried to play Tim "The Tool Man" Taylor (who doesn't love a good 90s sitcom reference?) and fix it. Much to my surprise (don't tell him—he'll never read this), he actually did fix it. "Someone" had turned off the heated dry.

Brady immediately accused me of being that "Someone."

"You can't wash dishes like that," he said emphatically.

I don't blame him for this accusation. After all, there were two of us standing in the kitchen, he knew that he did not turn off the heated drying, so … clearly it was a mystery. It would probably take the finest TV lawyers a full hour to wrangle up a jury and solve this puzzle.

At his words, I froze. I became unable to explain myself. All I could muster was to blurt out, "Well, I didn't turn it off!" I am an exceptional liar.

Don't judge my powers of deception by this one amateur move. I've got serious fib game. Lying comes as easy to me as breathing. It is a horrid habit to conquer.

Let's set all irony and sarcasm aside. I did it, y'all. It was me. I confess to turning off the heated dry function. It went down like this: I was washing some plastic cups and didn't want them to melt, so I turned the heat off. It seemed like the logical and adult-ish thing to do.

But in that moment, I was committed to a course of action. So I dug myself deeper into a Cascade-lemon-scented lie. I explained to him that maybe one of us bumped it as we maneuvered around my tiny kitchen while cooking.

Brady may have raised an eyebrow at my lame explanation, but at any rate, he let it go. We continued saving the world alongside Jack Bauer.

Later that night, at hour 18 of Jack's allotted 24, I confessed.

"I did it," I began to gush. "I turned it off. I didn't know any better and thought I was saving the life of my beloved plastic cups.

"Idon'tknowwhyIlied," I slurred as fast as I could, "but … I just did."

Brady forgave me (presumably for both the dishwasher thing and the lying, but it's possible he held a grudge over the wet dishes).

I breathed again. I was so thankful.

This small spat we had was the start of a snowball rolling down a mountain. This Dishwasher Moment became the catalyst for bigger and bigger fights. Brady confronts me about something, I lie, then I have to come back later, tail between my legs, explaining that this is yet another Dishwasher Moment. (Full disclosure: that part about the tail is a lie. I don't actually have a tail. If I did, I would probably be a part of a giant circus act and this book would have a free monkey that came with your purchase that washes your dishes for you. But, sadly, or maybe thankfully, I'm just your average girl, sans tail.)

It seems kind of stupid, doesn't it? It was the "heated dry" button, not a jewel heist, but that little lie and other lies are proof that I'm damaged by sin and badly in need of God to fix me.

And He is. God is refining me. God is making me better. He still has work to do as He molds me to look more and more like Him. I work against Him at every turn. I drag my feet (and pretend tail) every step of the way.

There are struggles we have in life. Not everyone's is lying. But everyone has something. When girls come to talk to me about their personal struggles, sometimes I can't relate to anything they're saying. My judgmental mind starts to churn. "You said WHAT? Why would you think that's okay?"

As soon as I can, though (and usually before saying something that could embarrass everyone in the conversation), I check my judgment. I take whatever struggle I can't comprehend and I rename it "lying." This ol' swaparoo charade that takes place inside my head while these poor defenseless girls are pouring out their hearts to me has saved me NUMEROUS times when counseling young girls. I don't always get their issue—but if I think of it in the same way as my own issue, I start to get it. Because I understand struggling with sin.

Too often, I use my sin, my fear of the truth, to make situations less awkward. I bend the truth or pepper "white lies" in the midst of my storytelling to get an extra laugh or to relate to someone standing within earshot.

Too often, I justify my sin. I justify my lying. It's the scariest sin to me, maybe because it's my sin, but it's terrifying knowing how easy it is and how it seemingly doesn't hurt anyone. I am so good at this that as years go on and classic "Jennafer stories" have been embellished, I myself forget the truth. I lie to myself and eventually I begin to believe it. … Wait a minute, maybe I am part of a circus act.

Lying is something I have to pray against daily. Those closest to me are used to hearing the sentence, "Hang on, I'm trying not to lie right now." My sweet red-headed best friend has to explain me to whoever is in earshot and has to hear this phrase (she literally did this for her brother yesterday—sorry, Phillip). Thankfully she (and others) pour their red-headed grace over me, and I experience small victories when I'm able to recall a memory, speak the truth without exaggeration, and not lie.

The biggest thing this sin has taught me is to be proactive. I have to actively seek Christ to help me flee from sin. Small sin, big sin, and medium sin. FLEE, Y'ALL! FLEE! Let us run as fast as we can the other way … because the scary thing about sin is, it starts with lying about a dishwasher and if left unchecked, it can easily spiral into a secret affair. Thankfully, God has protected me and my marriage from that nightmare—but I know sin is real. There is a thief that is coming to steal and destroy—so join me and pray against it. Let's be proactive. Let's actively hate sin. Let's gather our friends (red-headed or not) around for accountability. And fight. Fight for our sin to decrease and God to increase in our lives.

And for Pete's sake, don't turn the heated dry off on your dishwasher—your treasured plastic (FREE) cups will be FINE. ... Trust me.

CHAPTER 4

CALIFORNIA DREAMIN'

Our Branson home was a quaint and beautiful log cabin tucked into the woods. Brady had an office/music studio/spare bedroom in the cabin, and I vividly remember going into his office one day and making a declaration.

Actually, I'm not sure it qualified as a declaration since I spoke in the most sheepish tone possible: "Hey, um, lover, precious one, cutie pie … what would the possibility of me working for Disney be? Like … could that happen? Or do I need to let this go? Um, what are your thoughts … okay, nevermind. Dumb idea. I get it. No worries."

Very authoritative, don't you think?

Brady was calm and quiet (as he always is when I come up with wild ideas and crazy ramblings). He said, "I think you should pray about it for a month."

Brady knows me. He knows me so well. He knows that I've never been disciplined enough to pray for something for a whole month. Me praying for one thing for an entire month was about as likely as me training a raccoon named Bandit to make me breakfast in the morning. Spoiler alert: there is no chef Bandit at our house.

Hindsight shows me that Brady probably only said this because we were comfortable in our cozy cabin with our musician life and he didn't want to move.

But I didn't take it lightly.

I spent the next 30 days in prayer and immersed in my Bible. Or, as some Christians say, I spent that 30 days "in the Word." I've personally never really known what people meant by that.

I can tell you what it meant to me during those 30 days, though. It meant I read parts of the New Testament, a Psalm, and a Proverb every day. It meant I chewed on and digested what I read. I stayed focused the whole time I was reading. I concentrated rather than plan out my grocery list in the middle of Luke's storytelling. Although I can plan out a mean bowl of chili in the time it takes most people to read three verses.

To me, "being in the Word" meant making God know He was my number one priority during those 30 minutes. During that time, nothing else mattered.

This was all a new concept for me. "Quiet time," "Jennafer," and "studying" aren't usually found in the same sentence. Under normal circumstances, I wouldn't even put them in the same paragraph or book, but, alas, I felt a strong pull to Disney. And I was married (legally attached) to someone who didn't feel the same strong pull. So there I sat. Studying.

Those 30 days were special. I began to look forward to my time reading the Bible. It wasn't a chore. It was a gift. I loved it.

On the morning of October 11th, 2009, I woke up early. I walked down to a creek where I listened for God's voice on the finale of my month with Him. I listened to the creek. I felt the breeze and wrote in a journal (which I also don't know how to do, so I basically just scribble what I'm thinking and it helps keep me focused).

After my time at the creek, I walked back into Brady's office. And, just like I had done 30 days prior, I made a declaration: I really think I am supposed to work at Disney.

"Okay," Brady said, "then why do you seem so sad?"

He knows me so, so well. I was sad.

I explained to him that I had this vision of being faithful for 30 days, and on the final day, God would come down with a booming voice and start singing: "Who's the leader of the club that's made for you and Me? M-I-C-K-E-Y M-O-U-S-E!" Or maybe God would put a Minnie Mouse bow in the paws of a tiny woodland creature that would at His command, prance up beside me, and when I found the bow, this tiny divine fuzzball and I would dance together and then take a nap in a cozy hollow log. Or SOMETHING! Anything! I mean, I was faithful for the first time in my life with a quiet time, and God isn't going to reward me?

Lame.

"Did you ask Him for any of those things?" Brady replied.

"No."

"Go ask Him, and be patient."

So I did. I decided that a booming voice would scare me. I further decided that many woodland creatures carry rabies and I didn't need that. I decided to ask for a Mickey head in the clouds. Just three little circles. ... Come on God, you can do it!

I opened my eyes, sat on my front porch, and longingly looked to the sky.

And there in the sky, whether you want to believe me or not, was Mickey's head. It was a perfect profile, shading and everything. It lasted for about fifteen seconds, but that picture is seared into my mind.

If I could paint, those clouds, that message, would be the first thing I painted. Secretly, I'm glad I can't paint. That image is a secret only God and I share.

Beautiful doesn't begin to describe it. I wanted to shout for Brady. I couldn't find words. There in the sky had been a love poem from God to me and only me.

What a simple concept: "Ask Him."

My dad, Tim, has served my sister, brother, and I for as far back as I can remember. He delights in building American Girl doll furniture and preparing meals for the whole family when we gather around the kitchen table. He always made sure the three of us had the very best school projects to turn in. Our Halloween costumes won first place year after year. My Dad receives joy by serving and giving to us. If an earthly father can demonstrate such unselfishness and generosity, imagine how much more our Heavenly Father longs to provide for us in that way.

"Ask Him." How simple. How profound.

I felt so silly asking God for a cloud sculpture even though I am so quick to call my dad and ask him for help building my latest project. God provided when I asked. He gave me a visible sign. That memory is a reminder that I cling to. I think of those clouds, that day, and I am reminded to lean into Him and ASK Him for things.

Afterward, I sat, stunned, for a few minutes beneath the sky that had been God's chalkboard. I collected myself and then prepared how to break the news to Brady.

When I composed myself, I shared my highly unbelievable story. After listening, Brady said, "If you feel like God is calling you back to Disney, we can go."

"But," he added, "I will never live in Florida."

So we began to pack our boxes that night with California dreams in our hearts.

CHAPTER 5

HANNAH

When we landed in SoCal (southern California to everyone else in the U.S.), I immediately began working to get a job at Disneyland. It was work trying to get work. And I failed. I failed again. And again there was failure. This was followed by additional failure and was served with a side dish of failure (garnished with misery).

You get the idea.

After many failed attempts at getting my dream job, I changed my strategy. I began applying to someplace NEAR Disneyland. When you aim for Disneyland and fall short, you hit Downtown Disney.

I walked into the Häagen-Dazs ice cream store in Downtown Disney and got hired on the spot. Obviously I have that "can't go a whole day without consuming two scoops of deliciousness" face. Lucky me.

Along with working at the ice cream store and getting free scoops every day, I was hired to sell Sanuk shoes. I know it's an odd combination, but the owner of the ice cream shop also owned the shoe store. So being minutes away from Disneyland plus hearing you have access to half-off shoes will basically get a woman to do any job. ... I am "woman" in this scenario.

Into this cookie dough- and BOGO-era came a contest. One night as I was closing the Sanuk store, our manager came by and detailed the contest rules. Whoever sold the most shoes on the night of the contest won fifty dollars. That's right—the stakes were a crisp, green spendable portrait of President Grant.

Listen here, fifty dollars may not excite you. Maybe it takes way more zeros behind that five to get you to juggle hacky sacks in front of a neon green sign, exclaiming, "THEY ARE SANDALS, NOT SHOES"; but for my unemployed husband and me, that fifty dollars meant A TON. If you don't believe me, then perhaps you were not paying attention when I told you how hard I had worked to get to my dual ice cream-scooper/sandal-pusher career going.

So I set out to win that prize. I was not born with the ability to sell ice to an Eskimo. But great one-night-only-sandal-sales-contest winners are made, not born. I had one thing that had never failed me (well, in matters other than getting hired at Disneyland): my overly-teethed smile. So I scraped together whatever kind of charm I had at my command and I smiled extra big.

My enthusiasm was a 5-Hour Energy crammed into fifteen minutes. My smile was almost too broad and bright for anyone to look directly at it. Let's be honest, I terrified most of the customers walking into the store that night, but I sold the crud out of those shoes.

I was killing it.

My rival saleswoman that night wasn't even close to my sales totals. As I was ringing up the shoes of some fancy Australian guests whom I had lured into my shoe-filled web, I opened the cash register and saw "it." "It" was all the receipts from that night's sales.

All of them, every single receipt, had the other salesgirl's name printed on the top. None of the receipts were labeled "Jennafer." Heck, I would have accepted "Jen," or even "Jenn'i'fer." But no. There was nothing—not even a butchered version of my name. Each receipt said "Hannah."

Every. Single. One. Of. Them.

My competition had stolen all of my hard-earned shoe sales. Every sale I had won with a cheek-straining smile and an eye-bulging energy, she had claimed them as her own!

(P.S.: Her name is not "Hannah." I have a horrible memory and can't remember basically anything in life, but I do remember her name. Her name is seared into my memory. But to protect her from my mom and aunt stalking her on Facebook like lions tracking weak-kneed baby zebra on the Serengeti, I will just call her "HANNAH.")

After seeing Hannah's version of a pouch full of thirty silver pieces in the register drawer, I immediately went on break. I fumed into my scoop of ice cream (I consumed a lot of ice cream during these days. It was a necessity, and it was free, which was key during our months in California.) And then Pops called me. My father-in-law is no logic and all heart. He loves the most unlovable people. Literally thousands of people have come to know Jesus because of him.

His love for Jesus is only matched by his love for small remote control airplanes and his blueberry muffin recipe (which isn't so much a recipe as it is a jumble of ingredients thrown haphazardly together and then drawn out of the oven by the grace of God as the best blueberry muffins ever in history). He could sell ice to an Eskimo; he actually probably has. He is legit. That's all I have to say.

I told him all about my fifty-dollar shoe problem. I ranted about that stupid "Hannah" face who was sitting in the Sanuk store stealing MY money. In response, Pops proposed an idea that I'm embarrassed I couldn't come up with on my own.

Into my fuming and ranting and the white-hot branding of this girl's name into my brain, Pops offered this: "Jennafer, give her your sales. Go back in there and write her name on all the rest of night's receipts. Congratulate her when she wins the fifty dollar bill. The gospel is more important. Your name isn't."

The gospel is more important. Your name isn't.

So I did it. I didn't want to. I so really didn't want to. After that call, though, every guest I checked out got "Hannah" inscribed on their receipt. The drawer was filling up with hand-written "Hannah"s. By the end of the night, it even became … fun. Like a Peter-Parker-Spiderman-type secret that only I knew. It was better to write her name on the receipts. I felt a jolt of energy every time I wrote her name down. As the night went on, my heart began to soften and soften. If I was a Who down in Whoville, you might even say my heart grew more than three sizes that day.

In hindsight, I realize that was my favorite night selling shoes. Doing something for others fuels your soul more than money, fame, or success. Serving others gives you energy and happiness. If you become self-less, if you allow your own interests and wishes and desires to die, then in a way that only God understands, get this— you gain Life.

When our manager came to count the amount of shoes sold, she knew right away what had happened. "Hannah" knew right away what had happened. My manager asked me why I gave her all my sales. I should have responded that my father-in-law and a good bowl of ice cream can make me do crazy stuff. Instead, I said, "Because I

imagine that is what Jesus would do." (That is, if Jesus sold shoes …
and if He did, let's face it, you know they would be sandals).

I still haven't figured out how much the gospel is worth, but
that night I figured out it falls above a fifty. And that's about all
I know.

CHAPTER 6

CARLOS

When your parents talk to you about making your dreams come true, they never tell you about the tears.

It was 2009, and I had this dream of working at Disney. The main problem was that it was 2009. Disney was going through a severe hiring freeze. This was not just any hiring freeze; this was a Walt-himself-couldn't-have-landed-an-interview hiring freeze. This was an Elsa-creating-eternal-winter hiring freeze. Anyway, the cold was bothering me.

I was determined to force a hiring thaw. Every Monday through Friday at 8 a.m. Pacific Time, I would call Disney from my Branson, Missouri log cabin. Every day, I would beg them to take a look at my resume. Every day, at 8:07 a.m. Pacific Time, I would hear a version of "We aren't hiring right now. Try back again soon."

So every morning, defeated, I would hang up the phone and continue packing boxes.

In January of 2010, Brady and I loaded up a moving van and decided to just head out to sunny California and see what happened. We found an apartment that was small and charged too much rent, unloaded our Yorkie-Poo (having a Yorkie-Poo is what makes us a family instead of a couple), and declared California our blank canvas.

The Monday morning after we arrived, I woke up early. I was on a mission. I slipped into a black Juicy Couture cotton dress I had scored at a thrift store, and Brady drove me to the Disney casting building. I just knew once they saw me in person, I could win them over. They would want to hire me on the spot.

I walked in with an extra bounce in my step. I couldn't wait to hear where I would be working. With my College Program experience, OBVIOUSLY I would be a shoe-in for some of the most sought-after and coveted roles. Life was good!

I barely got up to the counter where a woman greeted me and explained, "We aren't hiring right now. Try back again soon."

I was devastated. I slumped my way back to the car and cried to Brady. I couldn't believe I was dumb enough to move our family to California without having a job. In fact, I didn't even have a rumor of an inkling of an available job. He held my hand, we prayed, and he drove me to Los Angeles and let me pick out expensive pillows that we couldn't afford at CB2. Then he fed me Pinkberry and told me he believed in me. Brady White, my friends, is the hero in every story of mine.

I told Brady I couldn't go back the next day. It hurt too much. I couldn't go back the day after that because my eyes were too puffy (I have the spiritual gift of "excuses").

I didn't gain the courage to go back to the casting building until Thursday. I walked in with my head held high and the biggest smile I could muster. And then I walked back out to Brady, got in the car, and cried. Thus began my pattern of heading to the casting building every Monday and Thursday, followed by heading back out to my car to have a good cry.

I got to know the Cast Members at the casting building reception desk by name. They probably remembered me because I wore the same dress every week and tried hard to hide the fact that I was about to cry. I have no doubt they saw straight through my attempts at tear-hiding.

This pattern repeated for six weeks. That's twelve visits. Twelve good car-cries. Twelve throw pillows ... okay, no, we didn't buy a throw pillow every week—that would be crazy talk. Who needs that many throw pillows? Me. I need that many throw pillows.

On a Thursday, I boldly walked up to Carlos—he was working the reception desk at the casting building and would be the face of my rejection that day—and told him I was there to find a job. He knew this, of course, because he had seen me (and cruelly turned me away) on many of my prior trips. He took a deep breath, stood up from his chair, and leaned over the counter to get a little closer to me.

"Jennafer," he said. "You've come here many times, and I personally have turned you away a number of them. ... What would you say if I told you I could get you an interview later on this week?"

"Carlos, that would make me so happy!!"

He actually did it. He got me an interview, gave me a card with my appointment on it, and sent me on my way. For once, I had come into the building with pep in my step and LEFT with that same pep. No slumping on that day!

I strode out to the parking lot, beaming. I climbed into the car and did the only thing that felt right at the time: I cried.

CHAPTER 7

CORN DOG JENNAFER

Every moment led up to these doors. They weren't ordinary doors. They were the Disneyland Casting Office doors. They were the threshold of the gateway to my dreams.

I'd moved across the country to go through these doors. I'd fantasized about my post-doors life. Here I was. My future awaited a few feet past these doors.

I like to think I looked poised and Mary-Poppins-cool when I marched through those doors. I like to think that. But let's be honest and say I looked every inch as nervous, scared, and excited as I felt. I may have been more Goofy-graceful than Poppins-prim.

"What," you might ask, "is on the other side of the Disneyland Casting Office doors?" It's an HR office waiting room, but MAGICAL. I was still a vortex of nerves when it came time for the series of short computer tests. They make you take these computer quizzes before you get to even see an actual human. I tasted fear.

Who were these unfeeling, computer buzzkills and why were they keeping me from the Magic?

One small misstep with the "I sometimes/always/never run late" robot torture quiz and my Mickey Mouse dreams would be toast.

It seemed eternal/infinite/very excruciatingly long before I made it to actual face-to-face contact with a person.

I believe Cameron was her name. Perhaps that wasn't her name at all. In fact, it is possible (likely) that she looked so much like Cameron Diaz that I've just called her Cameron in my head. She was the first face of Disney—my first eye-to-eye interview. Cameron was as tall and beautiful as her imagined namesake. Cameron's smile and manner quickly told me she was more than attractive; she was kind.

Kindness was an oasis in that desert of personal stress. After all, in her well-manicured hands, Cameron held everything I wanted—the magic of Make-A-Wish children dancing with princesses, the smiles of children of all ages, the costumes, the singing, the dancing, the joy, the tears, the...sheer wonder of it all. Cameron had a well-polished death grip on my Mickey Mouse Dream.

She asked question after question about The Great Movie Ride (my former Walt Disney World stomping grounds). Some of the questions I could answer, and some I just completely made up. This was the moment, though, when I finally began to feel something was happening. I finally had the opportunity to look into someone's face and almost sing like Giselle from *Enchanted* about how badly I wanted to make magic again. I sat in front of a woman who could help me reach my goal.

I was so grateful.

She and I chatted on. We sauntered down the Fantasyland of my past and what I hoped would soon be the Tomorrowland of my brand-new Disney job. I lost track of the time, and finally she asked me a question.

"Jennafer, what would you like to do for us at Disneyland?"

There it was. She asked me the question. She was serving up the Dream on a silver, filigreed platter fit for a royal ball. She was, wand-poised, about to turn my rags into a gleaming gown.

Seven weeks before that moment, I would have had a long list of requests for dear, sweet little Cameron:

A Princess

A Dancer

A Photographer

A Singer

Heck, even a Space Mountain ride operator.

That's not what I answered. Instead, I looked back at her (and there were tears, y'all, pounding the back of my eyeballs just begging to flow freely), and I calmly said:

"Ma'am, if you let me go clean the toilets across the hall, I will clean them so they will be more clean than the first day they were put in.

"If you would need your shoes shined, I would be excited to learn how to become the best shoe-shiner in California. I would shine them for you every morning.

"If your office needs to be vacuumed, then I will vacuum every square inch of this beautiful office.

"Basically, I…just want to make magic again and I will start in any area you see fit."

She paused.

Children were born, grew up, and got old enough to wear ugly Christmas sweaters (without irony) in that pause. And in that pause while my tears were pooling and my heart was thrumming, Cameron was thinking about what area she saw as "fit" for my passion and drive and dreaming.

At the end of that pause, Cameron decided where she saw that I fit. She placed me EXACTLY where God wanted me to be: food and beverage.

That's right—you heard [um, I mean, "read"] correctly: chicken strips, French fries, and corn dogs. Fountains of ketchup and ponds of relish. Hair nets and hot grease.

Being told you're going to work at the fast-food restaurants of Disneyland could be like a slap in the face. But for me, that moment when she said "food and beverage"? It wasn't a slap in the face. Are you kidding? That was my "and the Oscar goes to... Jennafer White" moment. I was so humbled. I was so grateful. Slap in the face? I almost didn't feel worthy of food and beverage.

I was going to be working at Disneyland! Get this—when someone ordered fries with their meal, I was going to be the one to make it happen. ME. Jennafer. I would be scooping up the fries. Maybe I would even be salting them. God is so good!

I couldn't believe it. Reading this, you might not believe that I couldn't believe it. My heart was full.

* * * * *

They trained me to work in three different fast-food restaurants in Disneyland. They handed me three extremely hideous outfits to wear. Guests handed me even more hideous insults when they were hot and hungry. They were not a bit patient with the little girl behind the counter, who actually had dreamed about the day she could put a lemon in their Diet Coke (their failure to say "please" or "thank you" was not part of the dream).

Still, I loved it.

I loved every moment, every shred of a bit of it. I came home smelling of French fries and barbecue. My Brady would kindly ask for us to ride home with the windows down, and not because he wanted to smell more of the Southern California air. I didn't care. I stank and I was living the dream.

Each day when I woke up, I leapt from the covers. I raced to put on my name tag over my Mickey Mouse-shaped beating heart. I was eager to meet every new Guest, co-worker, or giant-sized walking rodent. It gave me life to count up my register drawer at the end of the night and proudly proclaim to my leader: "I was only off by a NICKEL!"

Each day of getting to sell things like corn dogs was a joy. Corn dogs were my favorite by far. Guests would waddle in tired, wilted, and sad. I would plop a piping hot corn dog under their nose, and immediately happiness began to bloom on their faces. I held the corn dog key to making an entire theme park of people happy.

At the time, I was just loving my job, trying my extreme best every day, and selling corn dogs. What I didn't realize is that by being content selling corn dogs, I was becoming the best version of myself that I had ever been. Re-read that sentence, friends. I just wrote that selling corn dogs was making me a better person. It's weird, I know, but bear with me. I was growing into Corn Dog Jennafer.

Corn Dog Jennafer loved meeting new people. She was excited to get dirty and do the jobs that no one else wanted. She was humble. She was grateful. The little things, the small stuff in life, made her happy.

I never called myself Corn Dog Jennafer, but it's as good a label as any for the person I was learning to be. Corn Dog Jennafer realized that in order for Disneyland to create magical moments for

Guests, then those Guests had to eat. She realized that she may not be in the spotlight, she may not be noticed or even sometimes liked very much by the Guests, but she was NEEDED. Every task put in front of her was a building block in another person's princess-castle of happiness.

She worked hard, and she served harder. When it was time for a break, Corn Dog Jennafer would grab a few swigs of Coke and spend the rest of her break stacking cups and lids. She organized stock shelves FOR FREE. She couldn't get enough of the "serving people high" she was on. Who was this hair-netted new woman?

Some might consider it a thankless job, but I needed no thanks. In serving, I was completely satisfied.

I still would be satisfied, and contentedly serving up corn dogs, but that was not the last chapter in my Disney story.

I took the job no one wanted, but it was eventually taken from me.

CHAPTER 8

A LEMON IN A DIET COKE

One night I worked late selling skewers at a cute hut called The Bengal BBQ. The Bengal is just across the path from the Indiana Jones ride. A man and a woman came through my line, and we joked and laughed (I thoroughly believed it was my duty to make buying expensive food at Disneyland a FUN and enjoyable experience). They took my recommendations, and I fed them. Life in the cute BBQ hut was good. I remember the man ordered a Diet Coke with lemon. Lemons are not on the menu, but I was in the business of making dreams come true. I made his custom drink happen. I was on top of my game, on top of the world … the fast-food hut world.

As I slid his Diet Coke with lemon across the counter, we locked eyes, and he very seriously said, "Jennafer, have you ever thought about working in entertainment at Disney?"

Jennafer's heart stops.

I wish I could write about how calm and cool I was. I wish I could write how I laughed at such a childish dream. I wish I could write that I didn't even know what entertainment was. But I can't write any of those things. "Working in entertainment at Disney," as Lemon Diet Coke so casually said it, was all I thought about.

If only Lemon Diet Coke knew how often I thought about things like the Minnie Mouse Moment.

Many days and fast-food hours before meeting Lemon Diet Coke, I was walking backstage after a long shift. I passed Minnie Mouse. I told her I loved her. She blew me a kiss.

That moment—that Minnie Mouse Moment—was one of those unexpectedly priceless memories. You know how events happen that mean so much to you later in life, but at that instant you don't even realize how meaningful it was? Then, years later, you realize you have those five-second sound bites of magic stored in your mind and find yourself replaying it over and over. Don't you wish you could go back in time, stand beside your past self, and whisper, "Hey, pay attention. You're going to love what happens next"?

Minnie Mouse passing me in that parking lot was one of those moments. She blew ME a kiss. She was walking backstage and decided to make a little magic. The Disney Entertainment bug bit me hard, and I've never gotten over it (even to this day). I can pull up my mental clip of that Minnie Mouse moment as if it happened just moments ago.

So with this moment—and dozens more—constantly circulating through my brain, I got ready to respond to Lemon Diet Coke.

I looked him in the eyes and said, "Every day, sir. Every day."

He scribbled a name and number on the back of a business card and slid it my way. He said, "At 8 a.m. tomorrow morning, call that number and tell her I sent you."

The woman with Lemon Diet Coke lingered just a tad, winked

at me and said, "You really should call that number. He actually IS somebody."

After my BBQ hut shift, I went home and Googled his name: Sam Wallace. Google led me to Wikipedia. If we have learned anything from the inter-webs, it is that Wikipedia is the most reliable source of information ever created. So when Wikipedia said that my Lemon Diet Coke (a.k.a. Sam Wallace) used to be the Director/Senior Manger of Disneyland Entertainment—I didn't question it.

Just take a moment and reflect on how this all unfolded. I'd come to California—at a huge cost. I had arrived in pursuit of a Disney dream. I had cried many tears, sold many sandals, and scooped many ice creams just to get my foot in the door. Now, take a moment and look at how God was at work on that Disneyland night in a barbecue hut outside of the Indiana Jones ride.

God could have had me selling corn dogs that night. I could have been off work or on a break and playing on Splash Mountain. God could have put Mr. Wallace in any line to ask for his Diet Coke. I could have been too tired to care much about getting a lemon for his beverage. I could have been so absorbed in my own thoughts or dreams that I missed the chance to joyfully serve others. I don't know how or why it happened. But it happened.

I've never had the chance to tell Sam Wallace how he changed a life with a beverage order and a business card. So I'm going to take that chance now:

Dear Sam Wallace (and let me apologize for referring to you only by your drink order for several paragraphs),

Thanks for taking the time to scribble that number on the back of your business card. You changed my life that night. Because of you generously giving of your time, I have found a home in Florida. My husband has been able to pastor a church and hundreds of people have heard the gospel through our ministry. Not to mention, I've been able to live out a fairy tale and learned how to live every day to the fullest, not taking one minute for granted. Because of you, a ripple started in the ocean, and God has used it to turn into a tidal wave. To be able to tell you, "Thank you," is my greatest pleasure in life.

Overwhelmed,

Jennafer

I set my alarm for seven the next morning and waited restlessly until 8:02 to call.

[Sam Wallace is not his real name, people. … I don't want you to bombard him with e-mails and stalking his Wikipedia page.]

CHAPTER 9

THE AUDITION

I had been to the Disneyland casting office dozens of times at this point.

I was a regular—if we were in the age of Foursquare, I would have been the Mayor. Side note: I never got into Foursquare. ... It was an app where you would visit places, check in, and if you frequented that establishment enough, you could become the Mayor. Obviously, I have no drive to be in politics because I couldn't even be bothered to download an app.

Despite my failure at being elected the Foursquare Mayor of the casting office, I found myself back there again. It was eight fifty-four in the a.m., and I trembled with a mix of anxiety and excitement. Walking up to this casting office felt different this time. This time, I wasn't blindly applying for a position without any hope for a specific outcome. This time, I was scheduled to meet with a casting director for Disneyland entertainment. This woman held my ball-gown dreams in her perfectly manicured hands.

As I walked in, her smile immediately gave me peace.

It was a weird peace, a peace you really shouldn't have when you attend an audition—but this shouldn't have even been called an audition. In fact, I will refer to this experience as an "audition" from here on out.

I had experienced a full-blown Disney audition before (please notice the lack of quotation marks). Everyone who works there is very kind. Everyone who is striving to work for the Mouse is beautiful. With all the beauty and the kindness everywhere you turn, the intimidation in these almost-gymnasium-sized rooms is real.

I had been through those auditions before. I stood in the lines with the beautiful girls who looked like real-life cartoons. I smiled huge for the casting directors as they passed me by. And I kept my head up when I was kindly asked to leave and thanked for my time.

But this time, at eight fifty-four a.m., was different. This "audition" was held in a conference room in a building I had now become so familiar with, I could have been its virtual Mayor. The room was quiet and peaceful, and (against all the odds considering my current state at the time) I was flooded with joy and excitement. I couldn't believe Corn Dog Jennafer had been invited into this conference-room "audition" process. I was so overwhelmed and so thankful.

I slid into an oversized black leather conference room chair and locked eyes with the woman across the table. She began talking and explaining the process ... I think. I want to be candid with you here: I blacked out. I don't remember what she said or what she explained. I'm pretty sure she was talking, though. Like 90 percent sure. My first concrete memory is the way I felt when she slid a piece of paper across the table. The paper had a paragraph of text next to a picture of my favorite princess. She asked me to read the paragraph.

I practiced the paragraph a couple of times; I pronounced "betrothed" incorrectly (it's bee-troh-thed by the way, but who gets betrothed anymore, seriously!). She showed me grace. She brought out a video camera and asked me to try my best at a curtsy. I almost fell.

The fact that I experienced any emotion besides just sheer and utter embarrassment during this experience is a miracle comparable to that time the Guy in the sandals fed thousands with just a few fish and some carbs! (Sarcasm, friends. ... Sarcasm.)

I probably spent mere minutes in that calm room with that wonderful woman, but I soaked up every second (well, other than the seconds I can't remember). I remember as she thanked me and I was walking out of the room, I felt compelled to turn around and say something.

"Ma'am ... I need you to know something. No matter what happens with all of this, where those videos end up and what decisions get made: these past few minutes in this room with you has already been a dream come true. Thank you ... so, so much."

She got up out of her chair. She hugged me. She again showed grace to my sentimental self, and as she turned away, she gave me a final piece of information. She just wanted to make sure I was aware that I had just auditioned for a position at Walt Disney World (in Florida ... an entire United States away) and not Disneyland (a few miles from where I lived ... in California).

I was not aware.

Visions flashed across my cranium. I saw the husband who had just moved halfway across the nation with me. I saw that same husband who promised me he would never live in Florida.

"Of course I knew that!" (I lied through my big teeth that she had taken close up pictures of just moments prior).

The door closed behind me and I dialed Brady White as fast as my first generation iPhone would allow.

I explained to patient Brady how I accidentally had just attended an audition for a theme park on the other side of the country. 2,510 miles from the Disneyland gate to the Magic Kingdom park, to be exact.

Brady was calm.

I remember he said we didn't have to make a decision anytime soon, and we would just be praying that the Lord would direct us.

Everyone needs a Brady in their lives.

I found a nearby restroom and changed out of my audition dress and into my Corn Dog Jennafer clothes. I vividly remember praying as I walked to the Stage Door Cafe that day. I remember thanking Him for the opportunity to work at Disneyland. I remember thanking Him for the sweet woman I had spent time with that afternoon. I prayed for the people who were going to watch me trip on the video and analyze my freckles and big teeth. And I remember praying for peace for any outcome that would come from that room of decision makers.

I couldn't have been at work for more than half an hour when I felt it. My phone was ringing. I glanced down to see an unknown number and a voicemail from, "Lake Buena Vista, FLORIDA." I rushed to the backstage area of the corn dog home I had come to love. I tried to listen to the voicemail over my pounding heart.

They wanted me.

Walt Disney World was offering me my dream job.

Tears were streaming down my face. I shook as I called Brady. He rejoiced with me and told me he was proud of me and my symmetrical face! I was hesitant to ask, but I said, "What do we do?"

To which he replied, "Let's take the evening and pray about it."

I went back to my corn dogs and prayed with each one I handed out. I remember telling the Lord how thankful I was for these corn dogs and how content I was to keep selling them. I prayed so much that night … and I felt so much peace.

I couldn't wait to see Brady as I fumbled with the key to unlock our California apartment. I was excited to tell him that I trusted his leading of our family and I felt a peace about going to Florida or staying in California. If I'm with Brady, I'm content and thankful.

But when I finally opened the door to our apartment, I was greeted with U-Haul boxes and a husband who said, "Let's go on an adventure."

And we did.

CHAPTER 10

VALUABLE LESSONS

When we first arrived in Florida, I found myself surrounded (in a good way). Everywhere I turned, I encountered an incredibly gifted Christian. Think of it as the faith equivalent of the Grammy's after-party. Look, there's Beyoncé brushing past T. Swift. Paul McCartney stole a shrimp cocktail off Ed Sheeran's plate. Actually, Sir Paul's a vegetarian, but you get what I mean.

I discovered we were living in a constellation of faith superstars. Let me give you some examples.

Carrie welcomes people into our church with an enthusiasm and empathy no other human could match. She listens to people and has an incredible instinct for making anyone feel at home. Her hugs can only be described as legendary. She hugs so tightly and with such love that I once walked away from a Carrie hug with an ear infection. She may have squeezed so hard that my eardrum burst. I loved every second (except for later when I needed antibiotics and ear drops, but in the moment I loved it).

There's Amanda, who keeps every proverbial train at our church running with Disney Monorail-precision. She keeps the team organized, focused, and faithful to the church's mission. She's a taskmaster for Jesus.

I can't forget Holly, who disciples more women and girls than anyone I've ever known. She takes girls who are near-total strangers to her and somehow becomes their mentor, confidant, and surrogate mom. I have seen it happen over and over again, but I still do not understand how she does it.

Last and not least is Renaut. Let's pause here so I can answer the question you didn't know you wanted to ask: it's pronounced "rah-know." There's no need for you to be distracted on how to pronounce that while you continue reading; we don't need another "Hermione" incident. Did I not mention the Hermione incident? So, I read the first Harry Potter book and lined up immediately to see the movie. I was shocked to realize that my favorite character wasn't named "her-moan." Who is this "her-my-on-ee," anyway? I was deeply devastated. I completely grasp why Christians everywhere turned away from the franchise. Oh wait, Renaut. Back to Renaut.

Renaut is a visionary—gifted with the ability to dream big, effectively communicate his desires to a team, and get people on board with his dream.

These people were incredible, right? I only listed a handful of the amazing people filling our church community. These people, these godly people, unfortunately, were not inspiring me. They were the constant faces of failure in my head. I'm not as friendly as Carrie, I'm not as wise as Amanda, I'm not as caring as Holly, I'm not as inspiring as Renaut.

I kept looking at these towering figures as an earthly gauge for how great a Christian I was … or more accurately, how much I was failing hardcore at this "God-thing." It was tough. They were running the good race for God, and I simply could not keep up.

There's an obvious reason for that. I am not Carrie, Amanda, Holly, or Renaut (you're loving that pronunciation guide now, aren't you?). I am Jennafer. And Jennafer is wired in a wildly weird way. She's got green wires and blue wires that circle each other in a tangle and plug into a red wire and a pink wire. A Jennafer's wires resemble a sad cardboard box in the corner of your garage filled with tangled Christmas lights. If you could ever find the plug in that tangle, that box might light up into a beautiful rainbow of bright colors, but those tangles discourage a person from fumbling around for the plug.

I've spent some time untangling that mess, though, and I found out what I'm wired to do. I am wired to encourage. And I'm wired to love. Oddly enough, I do those two things differently and easier than others. I say these sentences with a heaping dose of humility. … It's taken quite the journey to be comfortable in the gifts God has given me.

I was recently at a conference where the keynote speaker kept driving home this point: "Add value to people's lives." I instantly fell in love with his motto, his life, and his passion. I found someone (granted, he was on a stage and I was in a crowd … but I followed him on Instagram, so it FELT like I had FOUND someone) that had wires like mine.

I was encouraged and inspired.

I wanted to know more about him and how he applied this life motto to his daily adventures (via the world of "INSTA"). I read about ways he dated his wife, how he enjoyed spending time with his grandson after school, and his daily texts of encouragement to his grown daughter.

I scoured his Instagram, looking for answers of how to add value to people's lives, instead of lifting my head up from my mobile device and looking into the eyes of people around me and seeing how I could UNIQUELY add value into their lives. (Full disclosure—I am typing this on my iPhone 8 Plus.)

I spent so many useless hours waiting to find my "spiritual gift bestie" that I could relate to, bounce ideas off, and learn from that I missed out on learning how I can uniquely love on people all by myself.

How could I add VALUE the way Carrie loves on others? How could I add VALUE to Amanda's overflowing plate of tasks and to-dos?

I'm constantly battling this need inside of me to go above and beyond for others to make sure they know they are important, wherever they are in life. That need to acknowledge and praise and connect with the best in other people can be killed or sedated by the soft glow of my phone. Most of the hours of my day are spent tied to an electronic version of the world. Instead of pouring out my love to others, I'm "liking" the digital snapshots and highlight reels those people put up on social media.

I have to admit that I find it hard to appreciate others—to see the gifts of God in others—because I find it hard to see those gifts in myself. Remember that cardboard box of tangled wires? On my own, I don't have the strength or the will or the interest to sort through those wires. On my own, I can't figure out how to plug in the lights.

It takes prayer and concentration to remember that God created me, He knew me at the beginning of time, and He has counted the hairs on my head. We can't encourage our teammates, our spouses, our best friend, or our children if we don't first realize that God puts value in each of us. We don't see it when we look into our personal mirrors of judgment, but in the reflection, there's an image of God.

So I wonder: how can I humbly value what gifts God has given me?

The answer the Lord revealed to me was simple.

I have to recognize and value the work God is doing inside of me. I have to value the grace of God that He poured out on me. I have to value the way He made my mind to work in a quirky, tangled-mess-Jennafer fashion. I have to value the heart He gave me that breaks for so many different issues in this world. And I've got to value the hard truth that His work inside of me isn't finished.

I began to believe and trust that once I opened my eyes to the grace of God, the gifts of God, and the mercy of God in myself, it was easier to value the good of God in others. Even better for me was the realization that once I saw the UNIQUE blessings God had granted me, I stopped comparing myself to the Christians around me. I no longer needed to stalk the Instagram of keynote speakers to relate my gifts to his. I didn't need to hug like Carrie anymore.

Instead, when I realized how God had intentionally made me in a certain way, I could focus on building a relationship I'd been ignoring. I began to form a relationship with my favorite Christian (hint: it's Jesus—Jesus is my favorite Christian).

So after this realization, after this fully hit me, I made it simple on myself. I found one person to value that day ... but then one person turned into two because it was just fun! I still struggle to realize that God made me a mess on purpose, and I still struggle to put down my phone and truly love people.

But it is a struggle and a battle worth winning. Each day, I force myself to think: "Today, I will value someone." When I held open the door for a stranger, I didn't do it because it was the polite thing to do; I did it because I valued their time and I valued where they were headed. Today, when I ordered food from a waitress, I thanked her genuinely; not because I had selfish motives for wanting to get my food faster, but because I VALUED her and her hard work.

I can value, honor, appreciate, and thank people differently and in my own Jennafer-wired ways. My way of loving isn't the same as all of the godly people God placed around me in this season of my life; that's a good thing!

Holly adds value to my life by discipling me and a herd of other crazy girls in my amazing church. Amanda adds value to my life by organizing our church and giving me grounded counsel for my whimsical requests (but as level-headed as she is, she is the one who snuck the snow machines in for our Christmas Eve service *insert imaginary book-fist-bump here*). Carrie adds value to my life by being able to be the extended hands, feet, and heart of our church when someone walks through the door for the first time. Renaut adds value to my life by encouraging my husband, believing in him, and enabling him to lead our campus.

I am thankful for that keynote speaker who hammered home his point about "adding value." He gave me a reachable goal. He gave me a simple thought that sparked something inside of me that changed the way I do daily life.

Today, I will value myself, because God sees value in me … because when He looks at all 5'4" tangled-Christmas-lights box of me, somehow He sees His Son. Once I can grasp that, I can focus outwardly and see the full value of others.

Until I learn to master that thought, can I get that door for you?

CHAPTER 11

TIMO

Let's review what we know about Mondays. There's a famous movie quote about somebody having "a case of the Mondays," which tells us that Monday is less like a day of the week than it is like ebola. There's that 1960s song that goes, "Monday, Monday; can't trust that day" so we know that Monday is a LIAR. Then there's that 1980s song about another "manic" Monday. And we haven't even touched the thousands of cat or dinosaur or natural disaster memes that feature Mondays.

With the stage set, let me take you back to a particular Monday and to a particular acquaintance of mine named Timo (like Nemo, except he was not a lost and traumatized clownfish with dad issues... that I know of).

Let me pause only slightly to tell you how Timo and I worked together. At that time, in the Magic Kingdom of Walt Disney World, Timo and I were in a show together. He played the role of the daring prince to my sleeping princess. We walked hand-in-hand on stage and we danced to synchronized choreography—we were a fantastic fairytale team.

Timo had worked for the Mouse longer than I had and let me sit at his lunch table and tell jokes that I thought were funny. That's the universal sign of friendship, right? I wasn't so sure. I always wanted Timo to like me and sensed that maybe he wasn't completely on board with our friendship. I had this thought that if Timo liked me, then everyone would like me. I would be liked. And that would be amazing!

Amid these subconscious swirling doubts of Timo's "like" for me, Monday happened. As previously mentioned—you can't trust that day.

Timo blew into our hair and makeup department and abruptly declared, "I hate Mondays." Now, you know that I am aware of all of Mondays' baggage. Mondays are not popular. I get this. But at this particular season in my life at Disney, Mondays were the days that Timo and I were partnered together. They were the only days that he and I worked together.

So when he said "I hate Mondays," I immediately heard: "My partner, Jennafer, is horrible, and I would rather be doing anything else in the world than dance with her for even 22 minutes out of this 9-hour day."

In black and white, several years later, maybe that seems crazy and self-absorbed. But, come on, you've never interpreted someone's comments in a selfish and bizarre way? Of course you have.

Timo's words punched me inexplicably hard. During warm-ups, people noticed that I wasn't being myself. I wasn't talking much and barely did the motions. My mind was the lead car in the Daytona 500 racing through every scenario, every conversation, every twirl, and every curtsy to see where I went wrong. What could I have done to make Timo loathe working with me? (Please tell me you haven't picked up on my obsession with people liking me by this point. … I feel like I've hidden it so well. … Oh, you have? Okay. Fine.)

But it was during that fifteen-minute mandatory (but, I'm sorry, useless) warm-up (and the NASCAR race of thoughts circling a five-lane oval in my head) that I came up with an idea.

You see, I realized in those moments of lackluster hand motions that I had a choice. Choice One: I could spend the next eight-and-a-half hours devising ways to get Timo to like me and determining when exactly he began to hate Mondays (read as "Jennafer"). Choice Two: I could spend my time loving my friend Timo.

I wondered if I could pick Choice Two and still spend my entire day sulking, because love is just a feeling, right? But I was tired of sulking. I needed a plan of attack. I needed to show that I loved Timo. And obviously that would include balloons.

I chose love, and I chose action. I knew what I had to do: throw Timo a Monday party. Then I knew something else: the party had to happen in 25 minutes.

I took a breath. "Okay," I thought. "Let's do this."

I ran to the front of the Magic Kingdom where they used to let us blow up balloons for free. In case you're curious, The Powers That Be shut that particular amenity down. I take full responsibility. So I blew up balloons at least once a week for a made up holiday—what? You've never heard of a Monday party? Get off my back, bro—it's a real thing. After arriving at our now dearly-departed balloon station, I got to work. I blew up dozens of balloons (I'm VERY gifted at being able to work a helium machine at rapid speed. … Alert the President, this could be useful to our country). In between tying off balloons and selecting colorful streamers, I wrote facts about Monday on brightly colored pieces of cardstock.

A few examples:

"Did you know AMERICA was founded on a Monday?"

"Chewing gum first went commercial on a Monday morning."

"Betty White was born on a Monday."

"Studies have shown puppies love to snuggle more on Mondays than any other day of the week."

Did you know any of this stuff? No? That's okay—I made it all up. Come on, people, I only had 25 minutes, a horrible internet connection, and I was in a secret balloon room (RIP, btw). Ain't nobody got time for fact-checks.

I paraded my balloons, my untrue facts, my colorful streamers, and my determined face to my locker. I always keep a bag of party supplies handy. Who keeps party supplies in their locker? I do. I keep party supplies in my locker. Imaginary holidays occasionally need to be celebrated, and I take my responsibility to invent and celebrate those holidays seriously. I must be prepared.

I grabbed a bag of candy, crepe paper, and some cardboard cutouts of Disney stuff and headed back to the break room.

Three minutes left. Three minutes until Timo came up the elevator.

People asked, "Oh my gosh, is it someone's birthday?"

"Ignorant fools. It's better than a birthday," I thought in my head like Maleficent, but didn't say out loud (because even if you're monologuing like a villain in your head, you can't say that out loud). "Today … today is Monday."

Despite my internal villain cackles, I didn't explain to my bewildered co-workers. There was no time!

I frantically tied balloons to Timo's chair until I was one balloon away from performing my own personal interpretation of the hit film *Up*. I streamed streamers. I creped paper. I decked

Timo's mirror with "facts." Finally, I finished with a kind of love letter that I taped to the door for Timo to read before he entered our break room.

> *Dear Timo,*
>
> *I know that you and I have had our differences. You spill coffee on your sweet new chinos and you blame it on me. You write things you shouldn't and hit "reply all," and somehow that's my fault. It's okay. Even when you called me "butcher-knife-wielding murderer of the weekend," I took it in stride.*
>
> *So even though I know you don't see it that way ... I've always felt fondly of you.*
>
> *I'm hoping you could give me another chance.*
>
> *Love,*
>
> *Mondays*

My preparations were complete. I sat down. My heart pounded. Incidentally, there's nothing like throwing an impromptu party by yourself in 25 minutes and pulling it off.

I waited. I could hear the elevator. I knew he was on it.

It took forever.

I waited some more.

I waited for a long time.

Then I heard it: Timo's laugh. He walked in and doubled over in laughter.

Everyone caught on and began wishing Timo a happy Monday! Everyone recited the Monday facts to him and added their own. Usually I don't welcome people one-upping me on my adventures of made-up holidays, but today was MONDAY. Today was different. Today, it was welcomed. Happy Monday, Timo.

He took his time discovering all the Monday love around the room. People handed him chocolate bars and more balloons and pointed out details like the "fresh and special extra-hydrating Monday water" in our water cooler.

He sat at his ballooned chair, still laughing.

We had so much fun that day. The whole cast loved Mondays that day. We laughed hysterically as we took turns coming up with new fake Monday facts.

I think of that moment, that Monday, and I'm reminded that I should never be afraid to make up a holiday. It reminds me how important it is to stop feeling sorry for yourself and to quit desiring people to like you. Loving others is so much more fun than worrying about whether they like you. I look back and realize that we should have more fun, share more joy, and love more generously. Why? Because on that day, in that break room, it didn't matter if you were as small as a mouse or as tall as a dragon; we were unified in our joy and love for one another. Silly as it sounds, we stood united for (of all things) Mondays.

And guess what? Seven days later, Timo walked into hair and makeup, plopped his bag down next to me, and said, "Happy Monday."

CHAPTER 12

NO FILTER

A million (I'm basing this number on scientific polling data) online "personality quizzes" ask you what superpower you would choose. Unless being Iron Man was a choice, I would choose the power of kid-speech.

"Kid-speech?", you might be wondering. But listen, just close your eyes and see yourself with the ability to just open your mouth and say *anything*. You can say whatever you want, whenever you wanted to say it. When these words spill out you will never feel guilty, ashamed, anxious, or nervous directly after. You (in your wonderful imagination world) have been given the gift of complete honesty! Well (surprise!), this is not just an online-quiz fantasy world. It's a glimpse into your past. You had these exact same powers when you were one-fifth your current size; you said outrageous and embarrassing things, and you got away with it ... for a while. Age, though, was your kryptonite. Just when you may have grasped the full scope of what you could say without consequences, you grew out of it. We all took our juvenile superpowers for granted.

I have great news for you, my fellow former superheroes: the power of kid-speech is not completely gone. Whenever we pass someone who still uses their tippy-toes to reach things on the counter, we get to remember and experience kid-speech all over again.

Working at Walt Disney World has allowed me a front-row seat to hear THE best comments directly from those little tippy-toed humans (and sometimes the grownups that accompany them). It would be a downright sin to keep those comments to myself.

So sit back, grab some hot chocolate (my mother-in-law has a killer recipe if you need to borrow it), and enjoy!

⁂ ⁂ ⁂ ⁂ ⁂

Sometimes, it can be incredibly uplifting to hear exactly what a person is thinking:

"Aurora, me and my dad think your music totally rocks!"

"Cinderella, I got your movie on Blu-ray. You're lookin' good in that high def."–*a very charming six-year-old*

"Belle, you should be in my ballet class! You twirl as pretty as my teacher!"

"Cinderella, I love you as big as a bounce house."

"Sleeping Beauty, your hair shines like the sun's rays!"

"That is your real hair? No way! Can I feel it? That's amazing! Seriously, can you tell me what shampoo you use?"–*mom of four boys*

"I'm naming my first daughter 'Princess Aurora' and my second son 'Prince Phillip.'"–*four-year-old*

"Belle, you know why you're my favorite, right? Because you never judge anyone by their appearance."

"I rubbed the smell from a magazine on me this morning, just for you."–*Chase the smooth-talking six-year-old*

"When I grow up, I want to be a character at Disney World. I want to be a real Fairy Godmother so I can wave my magic wand and turn you into a real princess so you don't have to be an actress anymore."

Sometimes, it can be … less than uplifting:

"Are you wearing dentures like my grandma does? Your teeth are very big and look like plastic."

"Princess Aurora, you need to brush your hair, it's so frizzy."

"Belle, you used to be my favorite princess…but then I saw *Tangled,* and WHOA—you're for sure second place now."

"Aurora, you and your friends talk way too much. I'm just trying to eat my breakfast."

"Hey, aren't you friends with Anna and Elsa? I like them more than you."

"Aurora, you have been in every nightmare I've ever had."

"This princess dining is awful—I would rather be eating with dinosaurs than sitting here with you."

"Aurora, do you like when your hair is all messy like that? Did you wear it like that on purpose?"

"Aurora, you need this five dollar bill. I can just tell. You really need it."

Sometimes, there are confessions:

"Your friends Anna and Elsa are so famous—my mom told a fib so we could go to the front of the line."

"Cinderella, I'm so sick right now—you don't have to take a picture with me. … You might catch it. I'm definitely contagious. My mom made me take purple medicine while I was in line and made me promise I wouldn't tell you how sick I am so she could take our picture."

"Belle, I really do like to read, but I just don't have time."–
Abigail the five-year-old

"Belle, out of all your friends, you definitely have the best soundtrack, and Ariel has the best hair!"

"Whoa! Cinderella? Weird. I thought you would be one of those robots."

"Mom's in a meeting so dad brought me to tea…then he found out how much it cost and made me promise not to tell mom we came here."

"This is my mom and dad—they were fighting the whole time we were walking over here."

"I've always believed in princesses until I met you. I now know the truth. You're fake. I saw the zipper on the back of your dress."

"Aurora, even though I'm wearing Anna's dress, you're still my favorite. My nana got confused because your names both start with A."

"I wish Elsa could see me in her dress today, but I know the truth. … I know she lives in Arizona."

"Aurora, do you want to know a secret? You know that stranger you danced with? It was Prince Phillip the whole time!"

"I have a hippopotamus under my dress."

Sometimes, it can be just seriously odd:

"I'll tell you how I know Pluto isn't real. I stuck my hand in his mouth, and I didn't feel one drop of saliva."–*Harper the four-year-old*

"My mom told me you and Beast played with an Ouija board and that's why he turned into a beast. … Is that true?"

You meet future entrepreneurs:

"Belle, I gotta take you to the book store with me. People just, like, give you books even if you've already read them twice. That's the best part of the movie. I wish people would give me books that I've read twice."

You meet extremely busy people:

Belle once hugged a four-year-old named Sam. He has two wives, three girlfriends, two kids (named Red One and Green One), and he works in airport security.

Sometimes, you hear about points of pride:

"I'm Carly. ... I'm three years old and I'm a professional songwriter. ... I helped Old McDonald write his theme song."

Princess Aurora: "I heard the most beautiful singing voice today."

Small Girl: "That was me, I was singing in my bathtub. ... Our hotel rooms must be next to each other."

"Aurora, it's very important that you see my very best curtsy. ... Just give me a second to set it up."

"Aurora, I want to tell you something that I've never told anyone! I'm not in kindergarten anymore! I'm officially a first-grader! I did it!"

"Aurora, I was just in my first dance recital, so it is clear that I'm a very gifted dancer!"–Molly the 6-year-old

"Yeah, my dad is as strong as Prince Phillip. He works out and lifts big weights. And he goes out of town for work, like, everyday."

"You always talk about how brave your prince is, but the bravest person I know is my grandpa."

Sometimes, there are questions or requests:

"Are you and Prince Phillip going to have kids soon? You would be a good mommy!"

"Belle, how does Mickey smile? He doesn't have any teeth."

"Aurora, I just need to understand one thing. ... Why did you touch that scary ferris wheel?"

"Belle, you have an apron on and kinda look like a waiter … Can I please just have a refill on my Diet Coke?"

"Aurora, be serious: is your crown made of cheese?"

Wife: "You've been my favorite princess since I saw your movie when I was five. That was 47 years ago. I must say, you've aged better than me!"

Husband: "Forgive me, Aurora, as I politely disagree with my wife."

"Aurora, you love birthdays! Will you come to my birthday party? It's snake-themed!"–*Paisley the five-year-old*

Sometimes, those questions are … awkward:

"Hey Belle, if it doesn't work out with the Beast, call my dad! Seriously!"

"Aurora, are you going to go home and take this dress off when Prince Phillip gets home?"–*Ella the four-year-old*

"You'll have to excuse my daughter. She's nervous because she thinks you're the real Princess Aurora."

"Listen Belle, I'll stand here and take a picture with you nicely, but don't get any ideas. I have a girlfriend back home."–*Jack the five-year-old*

And many times, it is obvious that Character Confusion is real:

"Aurora, I know your three good fairies! Aunt Florida, Aunt Merida, and Leaf!"

"When I grow up, I'm gonna work at Disney World and I'm gonna sign in little girls' books, 'Princess Ballerina.'"–*Cherokee the five-year-old*

"Cinderella, I'm your biggest fan. I love you! I watch your movie every day and I can name all of your seven dwarfs!"

Walking away from Mary Poppins:

Small Girl: "Mary has so many lambs."

Mom: "Wrong Mary, sweetie."

Mom of little girl wearing an Aurora dress: "Aurora, will you please tell her you're Rapunzel—all she has been talking about is meeting Rapunzel and I don't want to stand in that line. Just put your hair to one side and tell her you're Rapunzel."

Sometimes, the kid is just networking:

"Hey Aurora, do you think your Fairy Flora could introduce me to the tooth fairy?"

"Cinderella, do you have Jasmine's phone number? Let's call her and then we can all hang out together."

Sometimes, it's the most random thing anyone could say at that moment:

Mom: "I didn't realize Belle's hair was so long."

Little Girl: "Well, Mom, it's probably grown since the movie."

"Aurora, you feel exactly like a muppet."

"I brushed my teeth yesterday! They were so stinky!"

"Do you know God? Do you love Jesus? I can see your wig cap."—*seven-year-old Katie*

Cinderella: "Your Fairy Godmother made you such a beautiful ball gown!"

Small Girl: "No—I done bought this at Cracker Barrel...I LOVE CRACKER BARREL."

"Hey Aurora, do you have two AA batteries?"

Occasionally, there is advice:

"Belle, don't be nervous about dinner with the Beast. You're about to become a Disney Princess!"—*Vada the five-year-old*

"Mary Poppins, I know you're having fun right now, but promise me you will go back and finish college."—*a concerned grandfather*

And every once in a while, a kid will hit a little close to home:

My four-year-old niece, Emily: "Princess Aurora, did you know you're my Aunt Jen's very favorite princess?"

CHAPTER 13

A PARADE PASSING BY

Imagine you were just strolling through the shops on Main Street, U.S.A. in Walt Disney World on some random afternoon at 3 p.m. Suddenly, you hear a bright but brief trumpet fanfare. Then there's a second fanfare, just a tad more elaborate than the first. Then another fanfare and, wow, this trumpet player is seriously going to town at this point.

You go outside the shop into the jam-packed sidewalk just in time to hear a booming introduction. Booming, yes, but also strangely welcoming—like your grandpa calling you in to supper from the backyard (assuming your grandpa was a classically-trained voice actor).

"Hear ye! Hear ye!" Grandpa calls. But wait, there's more:

"Ladies and gentleman! Boys and girls! Welcome to the Magic Kingdom! You are warmly invited to join Mickey Mouse and his Fantasyland friends for a magical celebration in the streets. Dreams will come true, hearts will soar, and YOU will become a part of the magic. For the time has come to take your places and prepare to welcome the wondrous and wonderful Disney Festival of Fantasy parade."

And then the music swells, and you see dancers and floats and all manner of Disney characters coming your way.

Every day at 3 p.m., this scene replays itself. Thousands of Guests from all over the world stand in uncomfortable closeness to watch the floats inch by them. All usual rules about personal space are suspended. These people are mouse-ear-to-mouse-ear close. They're standing in the wet-blanket Florida heat with sweaty elbows touching complete strangers. All this effort just to catch a glimpse of their favorite Disney characters and the biggest and most breathtaking floats Disney has ever produced.

I may be biased about how awe-inspiring this parade can be, but I'm right, people. And if you can watch the steampunk, fire-breathing dragon roll past you without at least a little awe—seek help. Your awe gene is broken. Stop reading now. Go get that fixed, watch the parade, come back here, and I'll meet you at the next paragraph.

The Festival of Fantasy parade (just FOF to those of us who get tired of all those syllables) and I go way back. The first trumpet fanfares for FOF played in 2014. I was lucky to be a part of the parade at the beginning, and I have been so humbled to ride down Main Street at 3 p.m. these past few years. There is nothing like having a front-row seat to watch the childlike gleam in so many eyes when the parade passes. Some of those gleaming eyes belong to actual children, of course, but my favorite sight is when I see that same twinkle coming from faces deeply wrinkled from years of smiling. These white-haired children wave and blow kisses at their favorite characters with the same enthusiasm as the toddlers in their arms.

Maybe I'm sentimental about the smiles of older people. That's probably true. And maybe you think that I'm just putting a pixie-dust gloss over things. Maybe you're wondering if I only enjoyed the FOF parade my first few times through and that eventually smiling and waving became drudgery. First, you're wrong. I've never been smiling on the outside and angrily screaming on the inside (not during the parade, anyway). I've worked hard to be grateful for every day spent on a parade float. And here's why: it could end at any time.

"Princess" is not a lifetime appointment. One day, my managers will call me to a meeting and tell me that I've been re-assigned. I love my job, and so even the thought of it ending used to bring me to tears (but let's be real, I cry during car insurance commercials, so my tears are probably not a great measure of anything). Here's what a blessing it is to know your beloved job isn't permanent: you pay attention to the little, daily joys of the job.

Even if I am the best princess in the history of all princesses, even if Queen Elizabeth watches me in a parade and makes mental note of my waving technique, I will age out of the job. The certainty that my future in the job is uncertain forced gratitude to become a part of my work DNA. I am repeatedly grateful.

The lead pastor of our church once said, "Repetition makes the extraordinary ordinary, but gratitude makes the ordinary extraordinary." I keep this quote close to my heart because it so perfectly summarizes a feeling I get every day during FOF as my float passes Cinderella Castle.

So here's my own saying on how to be happy at work—I've kept it kind of a secret until now, but I feel that we're close at this point, so here it is: "Look at the castle and be grateful."

Every day, my float passes that beautiful castle, and I stop to be thankful for that moment. When it's 127-degree heat index and the makeup is pouring down my face, I am grateful. When I'm getting over a nasty sinus infection and just need to blow my nose, I am grateful. When I see a little girl light up as she sees my float come around the corner, I am grateful.

It's a simple concept.

Every one of us has something we have worked really hard to obtain. So many aspects of our lives are the product of hard work or countless hours of effort. Think back to the beginning of a relationship or a job.

Remember the effort you put into dating when you first met the guy or girl you thought was "The One." You spared no expense in hair product to have the perfect 'do, and you never left the house without mascara. You were prepared to bump into him anywhere, even a random Starbucks at 9:27 p.m. on a Saturday.

Or, think about the hours upon hours of essay-writing and standardized testing you had to survive just to get a shot at your favorite college.

What about that feeling you had when you first applied to work at a new job? How you hoped against hope to get a call to be interviewed, then how your palms sweat before the interview. Remember the feeling of wanting that job more than anything?

One last example: how did you feel when you wanted kids? Remember the prayers and then the tears of joy and just LIFE that you cried when you found out a baby was on the way? Remember the joy?

But then ... but then you got it.

You got your dream date, you got the admission acceptance to Dream U, you landed that job, you had kids (maybe not in this order, but stay with me here). You got your heart's deepest desire, and a few years go by, and it all started to fade.

Reality crept into your fantasy. The boyfriend bites his nails in THE most annoying way. The college is filled with gossipy cliques just like high school. It turns out the job is *work*. And one day, you're picking up the thousandth sock your beloved child has left strewn on the kitchen floor, and you're sighing, not crying. We forget that initial hopeful feeling.

That's when you look at the castle. You look at the castle and remind yourself to be grateful.

That's what I tell anyone who gets to have their first parade. I tell them to take a moment on the parade route to breathe it all in, look around, and be grateful.

I've always been fooled into thinking this just applied to people who perform in Disney World parades and shows, but God ever so kindly and gently (as only He can) reminded me to look at the castle and be grateful in ALL things.

So quickly I can focus on ME and MY DESIRES and MY WANTS and MY DREAMS, and the enemy wants me to lose focus of so much of what my Heavenly Father has already blessed me with and provided for. I have to take a moment, breathe it all in, and look at the castle and be grateful.

The best thing to come out of these moments of gratitude is the unique way the Lord has used my broken pieces and selfish heart for good. Turning my ways into His and my hurting heart towards the hurting people of this world.

No matter where you are in life and how far away you are from that metaphorical first parade, look up. Look up at your own castle and remember to be grateful, and somewhere in the world, I'm looking up at mine, too.

CHAPTER 14

A VERY SPECIAL VALENTINE'S DAY EPISODE

Brady and I were married on January 27, 2007. As far as calendar dates go, it's a great date. Those sevens make it easy to remember, and it's ours. As your experience with calendars over the years may have taught you, there's a unique quality about January 27th—it is that it falls a mere 18 days from another not-so-unique date: St. Valentine's Day. You've heard of it. You may know it as "VDAY." My guess is that for several years now, you have picked a "VDAY" Team. You either picked Team Loathe "VDAY" or Team Love "VDAY." NO ONE in the history of greeting-card holidays has ever picked Team Neutral "VDAY." NO ONE hears that "VDAY" is approaching and says, "Eh, it's okay." That team does not exist, and it never will.

Because our anniversary and "VDAY" are so closely bunched on the calendar, Brady and I have started a tradition where we celebrate Valentine's Day for others. It usually includes us staying up late crafting (Brady does the cheerleading, I do the hot-gluing) on the night of the 13th. After the gluing and Pinteresting, we make super-stealthy hot glue creation deliveries around town to our favorite people who don't have a valentine to share the day with. We have fallen in love with this holiday because it has shifted the day's focus. The center of the day is no longer our relationship. We are trying to put the focus on pointing our community to the ultimate Valentine, Who will never leave or let us down! We cherish so many fun memories from our late-night antics tracking down apartment numbers and hunting down our favorite singles. There is one memory in particular, though, that may never be topped.

First, let's rewind a bit. From the moment I met Brady, he has tried to talk me into learning how to play the guitar. He once went as far as sitting me down and teaching me a FEW things. For those of you reading this who are NOT on the single side of Valentine's Day, you know firsthand: learning something from your spouse is a humbling, challenging, and frustrating experience. Any marriage that claims differently is special. By "special" I mean to say "non-existent." Or, maybe that marriage does exist; it's just on the Team Neutral "VDAY," and their mascot is a real live unicorn.

Now that we have that established, let's fast-forward to some of my finest "VDAY" work. You will be moved. For Valentine's Day this year, I planned to surprise Brady by taking some guitar lessons and playing him a song after the clock struck midnight on February 14th. Please recall from just a paragraph ago how significant this was: my gift to him was to surprise him with something he's wanted and worked at for YEARS. This was a marriage masterpiece.

Now that you're on the same page, let us continue.

On the night of February 13th, as midnight approached, I asked him to walk into our room. I sat him on the edge of our bed. I then put the fear of death in him if he opened his eyes and peeked at what I was doing. I've heard threatening isn't a good approach to parenting, but I feel it's super useful in marriage ("Up next, my best-selling book about marriage advice!"). After the threats, I dragged a wooden chair in from our kitchen table. I tiptoed into his office to sneak out a guitar.

I sat down on the chair, placed the guitar in my lap, and told him to open his eyes.

"You have my guitar?" Brady asked, probably hoping I would have actually gotten him an Amazon gift card or something useful if I was going to go the gift route on this Hallmark-est of holidays.

"Yes, I do." I began to explain, "I learned how to play the guitar for you for Valenti ... "

That's all I could get out.

I immediately started crying, then full-on weeping, which escalated to heaving sobs into my hands. There were LITERALLY teardrops streaming down Brady's beautiful guitar.

I couldn't play a chord. I couldn't hum a melody. I was a useless, crying wreck.

Brady ran to my aid. He was understandably confused about what was going on. I imagine he was wracking his brain to recall the possible offenses he had committed in the past 24 hours to cause me such pain and agony.

Let me break in to the narrative just to state what will become obvious in a moment: Brady is patient; Brady is kind; Brady tries really hard to understand me.

Back to the sobbing wife and the baffled Brady. He looked at me and in his most patient, most kind, and most understanding voice, he said, "Sweetheart, what is wrong?"

I could barely muster a word, let alone a complete sentence. Finally, between gasps of air, I managed to explain, "I was so touched by my own thoughtfulness."

What must Brady have thought at that moment? He had been placed on the edge of a bed, threatened, and presented with a gift of a surprise. Then his wife had an ... episode ... of the kind usually reserved for singularly joyful or mournful occasions. And his wife's explanation for this outpouring of tears?

"I was so touched by my own thoughtfulness."

Perhaps it's best for our marriage that I never find out Brady's thoughts in that moment.

I can say that since then, "so touched by my own thoughtfulness" has become Brady's favorite quote in life. He can't legally say it's his favorite out loud because he is a pastor. As a pastor, his "favorite quote" has to be something the Big Guy said that was printed in red. But even if it is not his legitimate favorite quote, we have laughed so hard retelling this story to any new ears that haven't had the pleasure of hearing it before.

Marriage is fun. Yes, there are threats every once in a while, but mostly it's fun.

The fact that Brady can have fun with this incident proves that (regardless of my failure to acquire guitar skills) our relationship works. Even though we will joke about this for YEARS, there are a few serious lessons.

Serious Lesson #1. There are times when you do something for another person that is mainly a gift for yourself. The best gift in marriage is finding someone who can be totally okay with that.

Brady is my someone.

I'm a lot to handle. He handles it, though. He regularly wrangles me in and pretends to enjoy it. I'm thankful to be refined by him, to see Jesus in him, and to share his last name.

Serious Lesson #2. This story has come to mind a lot when I'm planning something for someone else. I love surprises. I love gifts. I love birthdays and holidays and merriment and cheer. I get wrapped up in all of this (literally wrapped up during Santa's reign over the month of December). Although this is stuff I love, I often think back to the picture of me crying onto a guitar, and I am reminded of what the person I'm doing this for would actually love. I've enjoyed getting to know my friends' love languages and what makes them know how much I care about them. Even though l learned a little guitar in Brady's name, what I actually learned was how selfish and self-promoting I can be while pretending to celebrate someone else. Compare that with what we know about the Man who gave those red-letter quotes pastors are fond of.

Jesus performed miracle after miracle—gave gift after gift. After these gifts, He practically begged everyone in earshot to keep it secret. He is the ultimate picture of humility. May we serve each other boldly, may we celebrate each other well, may we yearn and give quality over quantity and strive to be like our Creator.

That work of humbling ourselves may take years, but in the meantime if you need to hire someone who can play a mean song on the guitar (only) in the key of G, I'm your girl!

CHAPTER 15

MY FRIEND, SOPHIE

'm a mom. My child's name is Anabelle, and she is the cutest Yorkie-Poo you've ever laid eyes on. The. Cutest. We call her "moo," which as dog nicknames go is both confusing and cute.

Now, when I talk about my "momhood" with mothers of human babies, they seem to think that my mother-dog bond is not quite the same as the bond I might feel with human kids. Wait, what? I find this super hard to believe.

I'm not a mother (an actual mother). So I have no frame of reference. When people ask about my kids and I proudly report on the latest (cutest) antics of my Yorkie-Poo and pull up her #thatlittlestmoo hashtag, those people look down upon me with judgment in their eyes. I feel your judgment, people. The idea that Brady and I have been married for eleven years and have not yet created a new human being is a foreign concept to most people. But that's okay. Everybody is different. Some people have 10-year-olds by their tenth anniversary. We have a 70-year-old (dog years, people, I'm counting in dog years).

We are not against having kids; we talk about it often, but it hasn't happened yet. We plan to be patient and listen for God's calling.

Don't mistake my dog affection for being anti-kid. We love kids. They are wonderful and spontaneous and occasionally pungent. Brady and I have been blessed so far with 20 nieces and nephews! So we are not at a shortage for small children we can spoil with stuffed animals, or tiny snugglers who spoil us by curling up on the couch with us to watch *Tangled* for the nine-thousandth time.

To recap, I love kids. I just don't have any.

I am a Macgyver in the arts of aunt-ing, but dangerously inexperienced at actual mom stuff. So when people ask me to hold their newborn baby, my palms get a little sweaty. My eyebrow may do a little twitch. Look, babies are tiny tissue-skinned defenseless munchkins. They're portable but seem extremely breakable. I live in fear of being passed a baby. My eyebrow's a little twitchy just typing this.

This infant anxiety means that I am not a woman who has experienced baby-craziness. You know how when an expecting mom breaks out her ultrasound pictures and all of the women nearby do this kind of squeal-sigh? I don't do that.

Ultrasound pictures never make my heart pound. I get super pumped for the parents. I am so excited they get to enter into a life where they introduce this small gift of God to Jesus and also teach them that stoves are no place for small hands. It's a beautiful thing. For them. I do get excited. For them. But as for me, personally, ultrasound pictures are just grainy aliens.

Let me say that all of the above was true. It was true until I met Sophie. She changed everything.

Before we get to Sophie, let me introduce you to Kevin and Lindsey Dennis. They happen to be the two greatest people alive. They are smart, kind, and generous. They love everybody they meet. I can prove that last sentence: they've spent a good portion of their adult lives running around Walt Disney World making the gospel harder to avoid than a trash can (which, fun fact, can be found no farther than 30 steps away from any Guest standing at any point on Disney property). Kevin and Lindsey work for CRU (formerly Campus Crusade for Christ) and no one lives out the gospel quite like them.

Brady and I attended their wedding in May of 2012. During the ceremony, Kevin boldly worshiped, singing "How Great is Our God." He continued singing even as the most beautiful bride I've ever seen walked towards him. Their moving wedding aside, there are many fun reasons I became a fan of Linsevin (or should that be Kevindsey? I'm never quite sure how a relationship mashup name is supposed to go): they both love the beach and surfing. They have epic selfies in wonderful places. They laugh constantly.

I love Kevin and Lindsey Dennis.

When Kevin and Lindsey first showed us an ultrasound of their new baby, we squealed with joy! As noted above, my squeals were slightly less emphatic as some other squeals, but for Kevin and Lindsey, I was willing to exude a little emotion. They would be excellent parents, and the goodness of God was written all over this news! A baby was on the way, and we were pumped!

Baby blankets were being purchased, potential names thrown around, and all around the Dennis family there was the buzz that comes along with ushering a new little one into a community. In my head, I began planning the blog-worthy Baby Shower that would look so Pinterest but would really be 100 percent original Jennafer. Sometimes I refer to myself in the third person when party-planning. It's fine.

Brady's text interrupted my party plans: "Call me during your next break."

Nowadays, people usually just tell you things via text.

"On my way to the grocery store, do we need milk?"

"Meet me at Starbucks on Main Street in ten minutes."

"I'll be standing in Frontierland during the parade."

That's all normal stuff, but when someone tells you to call them, you know they mean business.

＊ ＊ ＊ ＊ ＊

I walked out into the hallway and called Brady. He was quiet and strong at the same time. Brady is great at being weird mixes of emotions when I need him most. He told me that Kevin and Lindsey were having a baby girl, and she had a condition called anencephaly. I would soon become sadly familiar with the term. Anencephaly happens if the upper part of the neural tube does not close all the way. This often results in a baby being born without the front part of the brain, and the remaining parts of the brain are not covered by a protective skull or skin. These babies, they don't survive. Some die inside their mother's protective womb and others are born and die very quickly after birth.

After Brady's call, I felt numb. I immediately sat on the floor. At the time, I couldn't understand what the condition was or why Kevin and Lindsey's baby had it. I wondered how long this precious life would last. I thought and wondered a thousand things, but all I really wanted was to hug Lindsey as tightly as it is safe to hug a pregnant woman.

As a church community, the news was an anvil drop. We were at a loss about how we could love Kevin and Lindsey but still ask questions when we knew they needed to be alone and quiet. Kevin and Lindsey may have been at a loss, too, but they began to move forward.

They named her Sophia Kyla Dennis. They nicknamed her Sophie.

I created a Facebook group called "We Love Sophia Kyla." I added anyone and everyone that I knew loved Kevin and Linds. I decided that however long God would entrust our community with this little life, we would celebrate it! We divvied up weeks, and every Thursday, somebody was responsible to celebrate Sophie living one more week on this earth with her mommy and daddy.

HAPPY BIRTHDAY, SOPHIA!!

You would not believe the range of ideas people came up with for celebrating Sophie. Some celebrations were very small, some VERY large, but every week was special and needed in its own way.

People planted trees with them. Sophie baked cookies with her mommy; she went on daddy-daughter dates. Sophie has a star named after her. My friend, Emily, made Lindsey a shirt that had detachable tiny princess skirts so Sophie could change outfits and coordinate with any princess she met that day. We live at Disney World, after all, so princess attire is a must for any little girl. Five of my most talented friends choreographed and filmed a beautiful dance for the family of three. And (my personal favorite) Sophie was personally serenaded by the members of 98 Degrees.

I started sending Sophie texts while she was in her mommy's tummy. I would ask her how her day was and what she was planning for the day. We would send each other emojis (both Sophie's mom and I were both learning about emojis at the time, and Sophie loved them!). We told each other secrets via text. Sophie always told me Brady was her favorite pastor (we had that in common) and she would always dance in her mommy's belly when he spoke. I fell in love with this little girl. I fell in love with the kind of parents Kevin and Lindsey were becoming. I pleaded with God on behalf of her mommy and daddy for her to be born whole and healed.

Sophie lived 42 weeks in her mommy's belly. When it was time for her to be born, family members flew in from all around the nation to meet Sophie. I've never seen a baby loved more than my friend, Sophie. In the weeks leading up to her birthday, we were all tied to our phones. We waited for the moment when Kevin announced, "It is time."

I will never forget the night when we found ourselves rushing to the hospital. My best friend, Elyse, was with me. You should know that for almost all of the crazy projects and celebrations I've taken on, Elyse has been the proverbial Bette Midler "Wind Beneath My Wings." Elyse is somehow able to serve me when I am acting un-servable, and she manages to love me hardest when I am at my worst. We drove together to the hospital in my light blue bug convertible, and she held my right hand tightly the entire way. We prayed and steadied ourselves for the moments ahead.

First, we alerted the masses, and they came by the dozens. It was a paramilitary prayer operation. People walked the perimeter of the hospital praying for a miracle, praying for our friend Sophie. We laid out blankets in the lobby and called in for pizza and bottled water. Confusion over God's will in Sophie's story overflowed into tears, and we held each other close when we cried. We listened to Hillsong United's "Oceans" on repeat. We sang out the lyrics boldly because we so desperately wanted to be able to live out the faith depicted in the song.

Your grace abounds in deepest waters
Your sovereign hand will be my guide

Where feet may fail and fear surrounds me
You've never failed, and You won't start now

We all were wading into deep waters with Sophie.

It's fair to say that the hospital staff had no clue how to handle the encampment of Sophie's friends. They didn't understand how fiercely we loved this little girl we'd never met and how willing we were to support Kevin and Lindsey in any way. We didn't care about their awkwardness or their disapproval. We loved this family so much, we would stop at nothing.

Hours passed, and finally, late into the evening, the moment we hoped for/dreaded arrived. Sophie was going to be delivered soon via cesarean section. There was some time for us to go say a prayer with Kevin and Lindsey before the delivery.

Brady, myself, and our lead pastor, Renaut, walked into the room with Kevin and Lindsey. That moment as we walked in is etched in glass in my memory. It was eerily peaceful. Their faces were brave yet so, so scared. I had seen them hold hands and praise Jesus' name so many times before, but it was different on that night, on Sophie's night.

They had to be exhausted in every way possible. Throughout the long hours of labor and delivery, Kevin never left Lindsey's side. Renaut, Brady, and I knelt beside them. We cried and prayed and held them. I remember laying my whole face on Lindsey's belly to hug my friend Sophie for the last time under the protection of her brave mommy.

Only a few people were allowed into the room with the tiny window that overlooked the operating room. "Only a few people" lasted only a few moments. ... After roughly seven minutes, the tiny room bulged at the seams. Every family member and friend that could be shoehorned into that space tried to catch a glimpse of Sophie.

On September 1, 2013, at exactly 12:28 a.m., Sophia Kyla Dennis entered the world.

We waited quietly (but impatiently!) for the "okay" for us to see God's precious miracle. The ten minutes we waited felt like hours. I remember walking back and holding Brady's hand, nervous/excited/scared/anxious to meet my friend face-to-face for the first time.

That room, those people, that day...radically changed my life. Through tears, we thanked God for the gift of Sophie. Amid hugs, we continued to ask for healing. Heavy and hot tears flooded our faces as we held Kevin and Lindsey while they doted on their precious firstborn.

We dried our tears as best we could, and we sang "Happy Birthday" and ate birthday cake. Sophie became the focus in every camera we could get our hands on.

I watched in sincere awe as Kevin and Lindsey proudly passed their tiny child around the room so family and friends could all soak in the immeasurable outsized joy surrounding such a small 6lb.14oz. baby. I don't think I've ever seen the sacrifice God made sending His only Son down to earth to us as tangibly as I saw it in that hospital room.

Seeing how unselfishly these new parents shared their baby girl, not knowing how long they would have with her, is something that still baffles me. It would have been completely acceptable and completely understood if Sophie never left her caring mother's arms. Instead, the exact opposite happened.

We left that night with so many joys. God was so good to allow us to hold her, hug her, pass her, sing to her, and love her. Even if we could see each prayer said over the Dennis family of three that night like they were lanterns floating up into the heavens, I am certain words and numerals would fail to describe the sheer number and beauty of those prayers.

* * * * *

The next morning, we got to the hospital as early as hospital rules and the State of Florida would allow. As soon as we came in, I locked eyes with Sophie's grandmother seated outside. In that moment her grandmother was putting on a brave face, but I knew.
I knew.

The next few weeks raced by in a blur. It was the strangest mix of emotions I've ever faced. I felt grateful and joy-filled for the hours with Sophie that weren't guaranteed, but grief-stricken for the years that were taken from her.

We planned a beautiful service. More than 800 brightly-colored balloons bubbled up all around our church sanctuary. Oversized butterflies, bright colorful streamers, and a worship band covered in neon praised God for the incredible gift He had given our community in our tiny friend, Sophie.

We had spent months in anticipation, we had celebrated, we had prayed for a miracle. And then we grieved. I believe that God did perform a miracle, but not the one we expected.

What I learned from that season of life was huge.

Lord, help me never be afraid to walk boldly into deep waters, into a tough story. Let me lead others to love well when love seems tough. Let me praise God and celebrate when all I want to do is cry bitter tears. Let me remember how Kevin and Lindsey shared their gift with us all. Remind me, God, of the selflessness of my church as they gave tirelessly of their finances, time, and emotions.

Although years have passed, this story is never easy for me to share. The emotions Sophie's name stirs in me are raw. It doesn't feel like the past; it feels very much present. The sadness is very real. But the changes in my faith and in my heart are real too.

And ultrasound pictures? Now I get excited. Every. Single. Time.

CHAPTER 16

FOR THE BIRDS

Being on a parade float changed my life. It gave me a sense of gratitude, but it also brought something unexpected into my life: birds.

That's right, you heard—er, read—that right. Birds.

Let me take you on a trip behind the scenes. Before that grandfatherly herald announces the parade and before that trumpet player gets his pre-recorded fanfare on, my fellow Cast Members and I are backstage counting down. Every day at 2:58 p.m., the riders of the first float are a little anxious, waiting for their moment. Dazzling Guests on a daily basis is not something we take lightly.

Every day at 2:58 p.m., just a short camera pan down and to the right of that first fantastical float, you can see a huddle of six little swans. Not real swans—that would be too much to handle. But three couples of swan-feather-clad waltzers who lead the parade all through the Magic Kingdom. The women wear stunning ball gowns that glisten in Florida's citrus-warming sun. And the men look so dapper in their suits with matching hats (complete Yankee-Doodle-style— I'm talking feathers in their hats folks—real, pretend swan feathers!)

The well-dressed Swans gather patiently by the float, awaiting the call to fly down the street so the parade may begin.

I'm not sure I can quite explain it, but I have fallen in love with these Swans. These Birds, or "My Birds" as I lovingly call them (whether they like it or not), flew into my life, and I hope they never migrate away.

Before I talk about how I first met My Birds, you need to know that each parade performer usually stays with its own kind. Birds literally flock together. Princesses chat only with royalty, and so on. At some point in the distant past, performers just aligned themselves into separate tribes that exist alongside each other in the parade but not quite together. Dancers don't dance with characters; characters don't pose with dancers. I didn't like this. It didn't feel right. This was not segregation, really, but I think we've all been in those situations where you're just not supposed to talk to certain people. In junior high, you sat with your crowd (be they choir kids or football stars), and no one told you not to talk to another crowd. You just knew. You sat at your table. You spoke to your people.

At the beginning of the parade, my spot on a float was *right* next to where the Swan dancers gathered. They were physically so close to me, but in that junior-high-cafeteria way, they were very distant. One day, though, the silliness of the situation hit me. So I just started talking to them.

It started small. Really, it started microscopically small. At first, there were just simple introductions. Then, just before the next parade, I came prepared with some fun swan facts to share. I started to say something to the Swans every day.

And no one noticed. The Swans hardly noticed. Most of the time they wouldn't pay attention, or I would only have one Bird listening. It didn't matter. I kept going.

As the leaders of the parade, the Swans were the first to cross the parade's starting line, known in the parade biz as the "sight line." Every time I was riding in the parade, I wanted those Swans to step across the sight line feeling encouraged somehow. I wanted them to feel valued, even loved.

So I kept talking to them. I was scrambling for bird trivia. I was making up things to say. I just kept talking.

Every day.

Little by little, as the plethora of three o'clocks came and went, a Bird would start to listen ... and then another Bird. Pretty soon, I had the attention of all six Birds, five days a week. They've gathered and listened through questions of the day, fun fact Friday, poems from the Charmings, and even a couple raps. (These "raps" were nothing to fly home and brag about. ... Just proof that this girl will do anything to make sure those Birds know how special they are.)

It's been over four years since I began in the FOF parade. Each of those days at 2:58 p.m., I have been given the gift of two minutes with talented dancers with beautiful hearts. You can pour a lot of love into two minutes over the course of four years.

Those two minutes, spread out over time, created a community that supports one another at all times.

We became a part of the same flock.

We call each other nicknames as an outward sign that we are one family now. I'm Jen Bird, and together all of us Birds invite others into the nest. The flock is open. No potential Birds are turned away. We cheer new Birds on nerve-wracking first days and salute veteran Birds on tear-filled last days. We celebrate birthdays, engagements, and a few months ago, we welcomed our first baby Bird!

There are even invented Bird Holidays like the annual "Love Bird" party at my house around Valentine's Day. Once a month, my household hosts "Bird Dinners," where we invite five or six Birds into our home for a nice meal. We laugh a lot. We encourage these dancers and build them up. These Birds feel welcomed and included under our roof, and I love that. They even call Brady "PaPa Bird." Just when I thought I couldn't love Brady White any more ... he agrees to be called by strange avian nicknames.

At work, no longer is the break room segregated. Dancers and cartoon characters sit together and giggle on the floor until it's time for "places." I sit right next to those Birds because they have become my best friends at work. God has made my heart so big for these performers, I can't help but love every single one of them. Last year, we made matching shirts (and sold over 60) that said, "If you're a Bird, I'm a Bird," and float-riding performers and dancers alike are spotted donning them to represent our Bird family and how proud we are to perform alongside such talented swans!

There are Christians ministering to the homeless, Christians ministering to orphans, Christians working literal fields across the world. We aren't all called to these massive challenges. We don't always know when we are standing on the edge of our own mission field. Mother Teresa famously said to do small things with great love. My mission field was a small huddle of Swans near a parade float, and I have tried to shower them with great love.

So far, I haven't "prayed the prayer" with anyone in the flock asking Jesus to come into their hearts. Most of them don't attend our church, or any church. I haven't seen much fruit from the relationships I've formed. You know, the kind of fruit other Christians ask you about when you're explaining your ministry to them. The Lord has protected me from being discouraged. Loving on these Birds is something I feel called to do. When I have the chance to listen to the Birds talk about their break-up stories and their big career dreams is when I feel most useful in His Kingdom.

Many of them don't know Jesus yet, but I pray as I learn more about Him and fall more in love with Him, I've reflected His love and grace onto these precious Birds. By the grace of God, when my time performing is over I will be able, with confidence, to say I never took a day for granted. Every day I have approached with gratitude and gratefulness. And every day, I've loved on a Swan.

There are Birds in your life. They (probably) aren't wearing fake feathers (though I really wish they were). But they definitely need your encouragement. Before the parade steps off for today, make sure you show some love to a Bird.

So let's go.

It's 2:58 p.m. somewhere.

CHAPTER 17

THERE IS ONLY ONE MICKEY MOUSE

There is no job like working at Walt Disney World. There is no other office where you come home at the end of the day and say things like, "I helped Daisy Duck put her shoe on." Or, "Have you seen my Insta today? I got a killer picture with Goofy AND Mickey."

I realize these are not normal adult sentences. I realize this is not a normal adult life. I am super grateful for my "normal" to be sprinkled with such exciting non-normals. I will never take for granted that my reality in this season of life may be someone else's dream. For all the magic of my job, I am most grateful for the magical people I am surrounded by each day. There are days, if I am humble enough to see it, when I am truly inspired by my fellow Cast Members.

Not too long ago, I was about to begin work in Tomorrowland, and I was not feeling much inspiration. My shift that day put me in charge of a few co-workers you may recognize including Stitch, Buzz Lightyear, and the big cheese himself, Mickey Mouse.

I gathered my Cast that morning and made sure everything went according to Disney protocol. We talked through safety messages. I made sure my "friends" had enough water and Powerade. This was all routine for me, but still the little kid inside of me shrieked with joy when Buzz grabbed my hand to walk out on the stage. (Eeeeek).

I met a new character attendant that day. Her name was Courtney. That morning was her first shift out of training. What is a character attendant? I'm glad you asked. Every group of characters you see at Disney World has a character attendant with them. As the Secret Service is to the President of the United States, so the character attendants are to Mickey Mouse and his friends. The attendants are selfless and kind, and they are mostly invisible in plain sight.

Attendants let all the love and attention flow to the character, but make no mistake, the attendant is working hard to facilitate every magical moment.

Here's what you need to know about character attendants: they have all the power. They might appear mild-mannered in their slightly dumpy costumes with ill-fitting pants and overly blousy shirts, but don't be fooled. They control every Guest the character sees that day. Be nice to those character attendants. They are the difference between "You're going to be my last Guest that sees Pluto today!" and "I'm sorry, Pluto needs to go find Mickey! It is time for his good boy treat!" If you are waiting in line with your three-year-old who has been jumping from foot-to-foot for 20 minutes JUST to get a hug from Winnie the Pooh—the attendant has your triumph or your toddler's tears at their command. Basically, the attendant owns you.

On our first meeting, I saw that Courtney was cute and bubbly. She had the kind of smile that you could see from a block away. She had curly, dark hair that she wore in a big, high ponytail (never trust a girl in a low pony—that's my life motto). To this day, I think she is the only girl I've seen pull off a character attendant costume and make it look cute.

I walked Courtney around Tomorrowland and explained everything to her. I've never felt more like Mufasa. Courtney was my young Simba. "Simba! Here! Soak in all the wisdom I have gained during my short time here." "Young Simba, eat the cream cheese pretzels, they are amazing and will bring you happiness." (I told you Disney was a magical place ... cream cheese pretzels being the most magical ingredient.)

My little Courtney/Simba project was going quite well until she informed me what her duties were for the day. She was assigned to work with Mickey Mouse.

Mickey. Mouse.

You remember Mickey, right? Of course you do, because studies have shown he's more recognizable than Santa Claus. This is the five-foot-tall mouse that color-coordinated families plan to see in August to get a picture for their Christmas cards. This is the mouse that every child kisses on the nose, and every dad gets punched in the ribs after he failed to capture the nose-kiss on his iPhone. There is a lot of pressure that comes with this mouse. Sometimes there is a lot of yelling. Many times, there are tears.

I tried to hide my fears and worries from young, sweet, and bright-eyed Courtney. I assured her that it was going to be an AMAZING day! Maybe I oversold it in my fear, but I tried to give her the pep talk of a lifetime.

"You get to help THE Mickey Mouse. Kids all over the world dream of hugging Mickey one day. And on this day, little Courtney from Texas, you're going to spend ALL DAY with him. AND GET PAID!"

I proceeded to set Courtney up for success. I made sure she was ready for everything the world (Disney World) could throw at her that day, and then I let her run free. Just like Mufasa let Simba rule the Pridelands, I let Courtney own her time with the Mouse. (I realize my Mufasa/Simba bit ended when actually Mufasa died, but just go with it. It's Disney, and we can get away with huge dramatic plot holes).

I walked my rounds that day with a smile on my face. Disney World and its Cast are a well-oiled machine. As long as you go around and pat people on the backs, encourage them, and tell them they are appreciated. ... USUALLY everything goes pretty smoothly. That day, I made it a point to have extra time in my schedule for precious Courtney. I checked in on her often and made sure she was aware she wasn't alone.

Later on in the morning, I was walking up behind Courtney just as a hulking, tall man in a red cut-off shirt walked towards her. He was not happy. I stood ready to defend my tiny and defenseless lion cub.

He stormed up to her and in an oddly upset voice said, "How many Mickeys are there, Courtney?"

My head reeled. I had coached Courtney on where the nearest first aid station was, where to park strollers, and to always carry extra pens with you for those forgetful Guests. She knew about water fountains and the nearest restrooms. I had put in an extra ten minutes to talk to her about the cream cheese pretzel, but somehow I forgot to mention HOW MANY MICKEYS THERE ARE AT DISNEY WORLD?

I am no Mufasa. Simba, I have failed you.

I panicked and began to approach the large man myself. As I was mid-stride, I heard the sweetest little voice reply back, "There is one Mickey, sir, and you are welcome to meet him. ... He's right here!"

I wipe sweat from my brow and let out a "whew."

But I "whewed" too soon. The large man replied, "I have heard this before, but I can prove it's not true."

My heart is now beating so loudly it is a timpani booming in my ears.

"Sir, there is only one Mickey Mouse, of this I am positive. I work for him, and he is right there!" said Courtney in a sing-songy voice, almost like she was announcing a new Disney circus act.

Is it over yet?

"No, I will prove it," the magic-killing red-shirted man thundered. "This morning, my wife and I were at Animal Kingdom when it opened, and Mickey was there to welcome us in. We park-hopped to Magic Kingdom, and Mickey was in the parade, and he waved to us. My son dragged me on Splash Mountain, and Mickey was at the end of the ride meeting with Guests. Then, my daughter has been dragging me across the park where we passed the show in front of Cinderella Castle, which Mickey was in, and now, we are about to get on Space Mountain. And here, right before my eyes, is another Mickey.

"Courtney, I am a grown man; please just tell me how many Mickeys there are."

My-heart-is-galloping-and-I-can't-really-breathe-and-I'm-panicked-that-all-of-Disney-World's-magical-powers-are-resting-on-the-shoulders-of-a-sophomore-in-college-who-doesn't-love Disney-as-much-as-I-do.

Courtney took a deep breath.

"Sir, what is your name?" she asked in her sugar-sweet voice.

"Mike," he retorted with a noted lack of sweetness of any kind.

Courtney paused and with her well-deep, big brown eyes, she looked up at the doubt-filled Goliath of a man.

"Mike," she began in her lyrical chirp, "you aren't going to believe this, but I was just backstage helping Mickey get ready to meet with all of his friends out here. And he said he had seen a man in a red sleeveless shirt earlier. He said, 'I saw him when I opened Animal Kingdom. I saw him during the three o'clock parade. I saw him when he got off Splash Mountain, and I think I saw him watching the show in front of the castle. Courtney, if you see him, will you ask him what his name is and how many of him there are?'"

My. Jaw. Dropped.

The sight of Mike's face in that moment instantly became one of my favorite Disney memories. His frown bent up into a smile. His scowling eyes squinted up in delight. His face began to match the color his shirt as the excitement flooded over him. If it had been nighttime, people would have believed the Main Street Electrical Parade was passing by from the bright glow of his smile! This big, burly, red-shirted man had become a kid again right before my eyes.

He hugged Courtney and told her she was the greatest worker Disney has ever had. He put his hands in the air in surrender. He looked her in the eyes as he began to walk away and said, "I believe."

I picked up my jaw and ran to Courtney. I scooped her up in my arms. I fought everything inside of me to not perform a full-on Rafiki-inspired proud dance around her in celebration! I was so embarrassed that I hadn't trusted her. She schooled me in the act of creating fairy tales and magic. I couldn't have been happier or more proud to be taken down by a newbie.

I told this story to the teachers of a class called Traditions, which every new and dreamy-eyed cast member is required to take before they set foot into their role at Disney World. The teachers wrote the story into the script. Now, every person who becomes a Cast Member hears a version of Courtney's story. A friend of mine who works in Guest Relations was practicing a script for a behind-the-scenes tour of Magic Kingdom, and a version of sweet Courtney's tale had weaseled its way in there, too! Chances are, if you work for Disney and you were hired since 2013, you've heard a version of this story. I'm here to tell you, this is what really happened. It is true. God had me in the perfect position to witness it happen. For. Real.

God whispered a ton of things in my ear that day.

"Hey Jennafer, trust the people I've placed around you."

"Quit thinking you can't learn from those who are younger/newer/smaller/less informed than you."

"Hey girl, quit being so bossy."

"I don't really even need you around. Just watch Me work."

I'm the type of person who pretends to not love the spotlight, yet always wants to be in it. I love attention. I love the feeling I get when an event or surprise gets pulled off just right and it's because of me. I trust few people with my plans. There are many times in my selfishness and my tight grasp on lists and plans that sweet Jesus puts Courtney's face in my mind. I'm reminded that I can't do things alone. Everyone has something God is using them for that I can learn from. I'm reminded to be humble. I'm reminded to trust.

If I would have gone with my immediate instincts, I would have interrupted one of the greatest Disney stories to ever be born.

Hey Courtney, I trust you. And you killed it that day.

ACKNOWLEDGMENTS

These "thank you's" are in no particular order, but I did list these people in the order in which I like them. Just kidding. Kinda.

(pleaze xcuse eveRy miStakee inn dis paragrafe. my amasing editer did'nt proof tHis.) Thank you, Andrew Bach. The only part of this book that doesn't have your incredible wit and wisdom is this paragraph because I didn't send it to you. In your humility, I know you would have deleted it and, with my lack of attention to detail, I wouldn't have caught it. You believed in me first, and I will never forget that. Your editing skills are top-notch, and I will never be able to express how much your generosity of your Oreo recommendations, humor, and masters in journalism has blessed me. As far as transplants in our family, you're pretty great.

Thank you, Brady White. Twelve years ago, you took a chance on that unprepared, 19-year-old and for that, I am forever grateful. Every day you live out what I read about in that thick book you keep on your nightstand with the small letters and tissue-thin pages. You are the best part about me, and I will never not admit that.

Thank you, Mom and Dad. You clapped for me when I would make up songs on our piano bench in our living room when I was in second grade. You only missed one performance of me as Sandy in Grease (because you were busy setting our home up for the epic cast party you threw). This book and all the shenanigans inside exist because you believed in me. Even when I invited you to watch me skate in the Olympics I held in our garage in 1994, you believed in me—and you awarded me the gold.

Thank you, Pops and GoGo. You're the reason I sat down and wrote this. GoGo looked at me from across the table and told me she would read a book I wrote and that's when I decided I could do it. Pops, you believe in me with the most fierce love I've ever experienced. You both love me as your own, and I've never been more overwhelmed with how undeserving I could feel. Thanks for raising the best person I've ever met, and for raising him to be the perfect mix of your best qualities. 143.

Thank you, Jessica Bach. I tell anyone who has ears (which generally most humans fall into this category) that my big sister is better than anyone in the world. You love me big in ways I don't even know how to ask for and because of you, I never have to ask. A nine-year age difference seemed like a lifetime when I was little, and I hope you know every single day, no matter how much of a punk I was to you, I wanted to be just like you. Thanks for always answering my phone calls—my home for sure would have been burnt down by now if not for you.

Thank you, Nathan Kinney. I'm sad for any girl who didn't grow up with an older brother. Staying up late watching "I Love Lucy" reruns with you are some of my fondest memories growing up. Thanks for spending countless hours making my hair look like Aunt Becky from "Full House." And thank you for not being mad at me for telling everyone how many hours you spent in the bathroom doing my hair.

Thank you, Aunt Sara. You went to McDonald's dozens of times to make sure I had every Teenie Beanie Baby they came out with, and your freezer was filled with Happy Meals for weeks. You also introduced me to Jesus. Those are the two best things anyone has ever done for me.

Thank you, Elyse. Thank you for moving to Florida when you only wanted to be in South Carolina. Thank you for taking the ideas I have in my brain and making them come to life in bigger and more colorful ways than I imagined. Thank you for not questioning my wild ideas and my short timelines. Thank you for knowing what I need before I even ask. I want every girl in the world to have a red-headed bestie like you by their side. I'm a better person because of you. (Mac and Maggie, thanks for sharing her with me…you two make my eyes sweat with how much I love you both.)

Thank you, Evan and Brooke. We live under the same roof even though we aren't from the same blood line, and you know when I have worn the same onesie a questionable amount of nights in a row. Thank you for doing life alongside Brady and me. You make us better. I love our family.

Thank you, Haley, Emily, Katie, and all the thousands (as Brady so lovingly says it) of cousins I have. Your parents made you listen to me sing songs in my living room, and I imagine they are making you read this book now. I'm sorry.

Thank you, Allen Kee. You were one of the first people I told about this book, and you believed in me and didn't laugh me out of your office. You told me Disney wouldn't fire me if I wrote a story about all my stories. Gosh, I really hope you were right.

Thank you, Victoria. You took so many of my shifts so I could make deadlines and write about our crazy life at Disney World. The way you love me and your friends inspires me regularly.

Thank you to everyone who has ever volunteered at or attended Mosaic at Walt Disney World. I love our church, and I love our community. My world is better because of the way you have served my family. Plus, anyone who loves Brady White and follows his wisdom is basically better than Betty White in my eyes.

Thank you, Birds. You put up with me crying regularly about how I feel about you. I hope you always know how proud I am of each of you and how honored I am to be your Blue Bird.

Thank you, nieces and nephews. I'm not good at being an Aunt. My Aunt Linda sent me stickers for every holiday in the mail, and I promised myself I would do that when I became an Aunt. I've yet to send a single sticker. Please know that although all twenty of you are sans-stickers, I love you big. Being your Aunt gives me a joy I can't fully describe with only 26 letters at my disposal.

Thank you, brothers- and sisters-in-law who made such beautiful children and show me grace that I haven't sent them stickers yet.

Thank you, Michael and Amy. You made this book look like it came out of my dreams. The direction I gave you was I wanted this book to look like a rainbow and an ice cream cone, but I didn't want a boy to be embarrassed to own it. Ya killed it.

Thank you, Jennafer (we have the same name…I'm not thanking myself. Although, I wouldn't put it past me to include myself in the acknowledgements, but I want to appear humble because this is a Christian book), Rebecca, Olivia, Carla, Julie, Holly, Lynn, Shannon, Darryl, and Emily. The sweet friendship I share with each of you is such a gift.

Thank you, YOU. I can't believe you've read all my ramblings. You da real MVP of this whole thing.

35772344R00059

Made in the USA
Lexington, KY
06 April 2019